Awake

Toni Reilly

DEDICATION

To all my family, friends, kids, partners, clients,
students and mentors who influenced me; and every person
who touched my life, even for a moment.

CONTENTS

ACKNOWLEDGMENTS

Cobby Vines, for your dedicated editing and unwavering loyalty I am grateful. Bebe Majstorovic, Liz Formosa, Christel Christensen, Caitlin Gardan and Megan Hallifax, you all contributed to the compilation, objective counseling and editing of Awake. Ralph Brogden, because of you this is out there. My heartfelt thanks to you all.

PREFACE

This book took more than ten years to complete. I beat myself up often for lacking the motivation to write. The reality is, there was so much more I had to live through before I could finish it. When I began writing, I had a different outlook on life, having not yet reached the understanding that I agreed to everything. In the beginning I had not yet recalled that my soul chose my parents who agreed to play a role in every interaction which transpired throughout my life. I had to rewrite some of my story to centre it around me, rather than blaming or attacking anyone else. There were stories where I mentioned others, some of whom I was holding accountable for my feelings, rather than seeing them as volunteers, assisting me through my experiential script as Toni Reilly. Universal timing overruled my will.

My navigation through life saw me evolve from a small town girl who married, divorced, then travelled the world studying human nature and researching therapeutic techniques. I developed methods and the means to teach the profoundly simple concepts I uncovered. I achieved all this while raising three children. My personal evolution emerged through euphoria, grief, love and heartbreak - all of which impacted my tolerance of culture and perspective of humanity. I was privileged to first-hand insights shared by the many individuals who trusted me enough to reveal their flaws. I had to acknowledge my own as well.

Now that I am out the other side, less bruised and a lot wiser,

I yearn to share my story: how I arrived here, from childhood through my thirties, on to the liberating wake-up call which followed loads of personal development.

From the age of fifteen I had a feeling there was purpose to my life, in my heart I knew that I was somehow supposed to work with people. The confusion for me was that I was under the impression I already was, since I worked in retail at that time. That feeling persisted, popping into my thoughts randomly, until I was thirty-five, when finally I received a clear glimpse of where I was headed - which was, indeed, working with people.

It is hard to imagine that today I am leading an entirely different life than how I imagined. The person I am now, compared to before, is in some ways barely recognizable, even to myself. Being divorced, raising three children on my own, working as an intuitive therapist in my own practice, developing my own unique modality of therapy, writing and speaking in public, are not things I envisaged. My fated life map guided me in a unique whirlwind direction ever since.

Coming out of obscurity took time, courage and relentless drive. Some days were up and some down. Was it easy? Not always. Fun? Often. Sad? Sometimes intensely so. Confusion reigned many times, though clarity always lurked in the background, waiting for my new improved perspective to sink in.

I had many breakthrough moments. The harshest of all were the times when I believed I had overcome something, then realising I had fallen back. Those were the moments where I felt like smacking my forehead. Each time I broke through, I was tested again, just to be sure I really had it. Often I had grasped my test, whereas other times I became aware of what I was doing to impede myself faster than before.

It was always confronting being assured that no one else was at fault, and everything I did or said was about me. I arrived at my revelations in my own sweet time. I was a bit of a slow learner, but hey, I made it and I am still here being tested. Perhaps my biggest epiphany of all was defining that everyone is here doing their own thing. Nothing can be forced on any person. A life plan is far stronger than my human need to control by suggestion or subtle manipulation of what I feel it the best thing for someone, and this includes my children.

Realising that I was a control freak, at least to a certain extent, cracked me up! When this fact was in my face I literally burst into laughter, as I believed I was nothing of the sort. Wanting what is 'best' for a teenage child is controlling them. If it is indeed what is 'best,' based on their personality, they will not resist and there will be very little tension. Children and teenagers have distinct personalities and lives to carry out. We immediately begin to shape our children to fit the status quo (whatever that is within the culture we are raised) as soon as they are born.

I believed people were complex, individual enigmas unable to be fully understood; because this was how I used to feel. I discovered humanity is quite the opposite: with one constant being, each person experiences feelings and emotions the same way. What triggers our feelings is not standard; different experiences create emotional reactions of varying depths, person-to-person.

Knowing that we are all innately programmed, by nature and design, provides an opportunity to gain insight into who we are at the core. Accessing information about the psyche of an individual allows for detailed comprehension of their inner workings. This knowledge facilitates tolerance of our own innate behaviours and idiosyncrasies.

If we were taught at an early age in school about our personality traits, our challenges, and incredible potential, we would be less likely to end up forced into a career that did not suit us or attempt to push against our natural way of being. Influences from people such as parents, teachers, friends and relatives would no longer direct people into something they are simply not cut out for. Imagine having the inside knowledge of which areas in life we may potentially excel in. That means failure is taken out of the equation. It does not exist, where in reality, what is often viewed as failure is merely a timely block designed to redirect us toward another opportunity.

This solution may contradict life purpose, at least in my generation and many before me. You see, if our life map requires, we will be forced to go against our innate traits and the script will include circumstances to lose and regain clarity. Another term for seeking personal absolution is *soul searching*. Though it is not our soul we are searching for; it is the innate personality we were born with, the psyche [spirit] of who we are incarnated as right now, here on Earth.

Soul energy is omnipresent, pure and fully unconditional, neither less nor more than any other soul, devoid of all human initiated perception of hierarchy, linear time, knowledge or dogma.

Every person is born with a unique blueprint, I call it a *SoulLife™ Map*. This pre-determined outline can be interpreted using the date, time and town of birth, as well as the energy of our name. This information provides acute detail of one's mission in life, including strategies to navigate through. An intuitive or someone with psychic ability can tune into the energy of a living person and provide insight, guidance, and affirmation from snippets of their plan, which is held within the confines of our energy field. Individuals are able to access this information themselves; they need only learn to be still enough to sense energy.

Intuition is one of my strong points. By using it for myself and others it became stronger as I discovered how to listen and interpret in my unique way. Utilising intuition directed me seamlessly on my soul mission. We are all intuitive; each and every person incarnated is a unique combination of energy originating from intelligent, all-knowing, unconditional collective energy, which is our soul.

I feel certain that we cannot let go of someone or memories until our map runs its predestined course. Natural attrition takes place, it overrides our mind, or well-meaning therapists or friends advising us to let go and move on. Until we work through our process and reach that stage for ourselves it will be impossible to let go. Failure is impossible, we are simply living.

Forgiving others is something we do unconsciously. It happens naturally, just the same as letting go – both reveal symptoms of peace, which is felt as opposed to an action we take. When we arrive, there is this feeling of contentment determining that we have earned the marks: an A for acceptance, B for benevolence or C for compassion.

We are kind and do nice things for others because it makes us feel good about ourselves. Standing up for people creates a feeling of worthiness. When we deny our own needs by busying ourselves with those of others, gradually we inadvertently diminish personal self-worth. Self-worth is the key driver silently maneuvering our behaviour. Life eventually forces us to acquire a balance where we feel good enough about who we are, and this difficult process demands our attention, apathy, kindness, assertion and discernment.

Karma is not payback; rather, it is the opportunity to experience the many aspects of living. People often use it as a scapegoat, with karma copping the blame when life gets tough. Occasionally someone will say something like, "I must have been a terrible person in my last life for this to happen to me." Karma is not a debt either; we do not accrue a list of things we have to pay back in the next incarnation. Each experience we have here is outlined; we must know all sides of any experience to comprehend fully. For example, if we are the victim of an abusive act, either in this life or another we will at some stage be the perpetrator. These are all human experiences. Good and bad do not exist and we are not punished when we leave our body.

We arrive into this world alone, and we will leave alone. At death, our immortal soul transitions back to the energetic oasis of equal co-existence, free from restraints of a human body and man-made doctrines. The purpose which eluded us while living is revealed.

Life is no longer a struggle. I am comfortable showing when I feel vulnerable and I am at ease with the constant ebb and flow; however, drama no longer exists, as I see life happening for me, not to me.

At this juncture, l am almost an empty-nester. It is more than eleven years since my marriage split and a couple of years being without a partner. My ex-husband still does not communicate with me, my children walk on eggshells at the thought of us being in the same room, or passing one another in the street. That is a burden for them to live with. I raised my kids on my own, with little support. I earned just enough money to keep us afloat. Thank goodness for my credit card, which has been maxed out many times. I have travelled the world and my country raising awareness of my work and seeing clients. I am happy with the job I have done.

By dissecting my life, I hope to spell out in a way that resonates the not-so-intricate intricacies of what I believe to be the meaning of life.

My overall philosophy and belief is that life on Earth is an experiment directed by a carefully scripted and meticulously planned venture, allowing our already-pure, unconditional soul to experience pleasure and pain - which a physical body can facilitate. Touch, taste, sound, movement, intimacy are all treasures to encounter while incarnated as we experience the gamut of emotions in all their glory and trauma.

My life to date is the premise for developing my visionary concept, SoulLife™ Coaching. The modality is derived from the make-up we each consist of while incarnated.

SOUL	LIFE
Intuition	Will and Ego
Guidance	Logic and common sense
Wisdom	Knowledge
Unconditional	Conditional
Sixth sense	PhysicalSenses

The smoothest way to live involves accepting the existence of both aspects. Disparities between soul and life energies are the reason we struggle.

In this book I share my stories and what I discovered through personal experiences; how I received clarity around my own challenges and how my beliefs and understanding of life emerged through my professional passion. Having facilitated thousands of people to recall past life memories or visit the soul life area where we are pure energy unrestricted by doctrines dictated by culture, society or religion, I can comprehend why we return in different bodies to live through encounters in life.

I am delighted to have you to join me in discovering what life is all about. My hope is that it gives you a wonderful new perspective on yourself and the way of the world.

CHAPTER 1:
WHY ARE YOU HERE?

Reincarnation is the concept that we return more than once to experience life on Earth as a human being. Each incarnation is outlined by a predetermined plan, ensuring a great selection of lifetimes in order to experience the main aspects of being a person. Reincarnation forms a large part of my philosophy for why we are here and what the purpose of life is. What would be the point in enduring hardship, if at the end of our lives we die and it is all over, or that this life is the one and only chance we get? Why would some have easy lives, and others harsh ones? I have determined that no life is necessarily easy - the notion that some are is judged by our perception. Every individual is here addressing varying degrees of confrontation. No matter what demographic, culture, or colour, financial means or quality of life, be assured we all have something to encounter. Often the circumstances we perceive to be the harshest are not, and those we believe have it easy are enduring the hardest – it hinges on the individual. The polarities in circumstances are surprising. At some stage every single one of us will be challenged by life.

What is your biggest fear? Is it spiders, snakes or dogs? Is it heights? Is it being alone or that people might not like you? Is it that you are not good enough? It is likely that, as with the majority of humanity, our greatest fear is of death. Hence the fear of spiders, snakes, or dogs. What if they bite us? We might get an infection and die. Death anxiety plays a part in many people's lives, weaving its unrealised intention, manipulating our psyche.

Because we fear dying, we buy products and services which claim to make us healthier, younger and more vital so we can avoid illness and live longer. Consumerism is the beneficiary of our deepest fear.

The evolution of humanity is shifting collectively, as one by one we individually take action to free ourselves from reacting to fear. We get to make a choice to address the underlying emotion and be liberated from the existential anxiety, which lurks with no real basis, except from a perception we developed to protect ourselves from our fears in the first place.

In practical terms this means that the behaviours we developed to cover up fears (insecurities) and perceived flaws are presented back to us - in our face, so to speak - allowing us to become aware of what we do, and most importantly, why we do it. This opens us up to two powerful options: to either take action by adjusting our reaction, or to simply accept ourselves just the way that we are. What kind of behaviours? The list is long, but consider these as examples. Things like: continually seeking validation, being overly loud or quiet, codependence, manipulating outcomes, people-pleasing, being super busy, always being around people, preferring not to be alone, controlling partners, children, colleagues and ourselves.

Each of us has our own intrinsically connected mentor and counsellor with the best intentions and advice for us. I believe this to be our higher self, the energy also known as our soul. The person that you are now represents your soul. Only a portion of our entire soul energy is in the body that we currently occupy during this round at the School of Life. There is no need for any guru or organisation to improve us or to make us whole because we already are. By communicating with our soul we are assured of that.

Through careful consideration validated by my research, I believe that the major experiences we have in our lives are planned, and we agree to the outline before we are born. The words destiny or fate are often used to describe this idea. Returning to life again and again is how we experience each side of any circumstance. Wealthy/poor; angry/calm; partnered/not partnered; abuser/abused; male/female; healthy/unhealthy; dependable/codependent - notice the polarities.

For example, in one life we may be viewed by our child as a distant, self-absorbed parent and then in another lifetime be the child of a similar-natured parent. Despite how we might be viewed by one or more people in our lives, opinion is derived from their perception and does not make us bad. Every person is here on a mission, and the most life changing attitude we master is to resist assigning blame.

Karma is neither payback or punishment. It facilitates the option to experience all sides of any human situation. In this case, to accept the parent as they are. Through acceptance we navigate challenging moments as an opportunity to learn by experience as a willing participant, not a victim. The student role does not mean that we must forgive or condone cruel, humiliating, vindictive, disturbing or heartbreaking things that have happened. However, if we are unable to eventually reach acceptance for each challenge, it is, unfortunately, *we* who will suffer the emotions, not the offender.

Recall when you have felt furious at the way another person treated you. Sad, when someone hurt you. Devastated by the choice of another. Disappointed or humiliated by someone else's actions. Ashamed of your heritage. Guilty for events and outcomes which were not in your control, or desires that were. Harbouring memories, dwelling and reliving intense emotions, is how *you* suffer, not them. Resist blame; otherwise, nothing changes, as you remain captive to the less-than-favourable thoughts that keep you in a holding pattern.

I believe all experiences are planned, forcing us to feel by living through a wide and varied range of emotions. Feelings are what matter most; any story we tell loses impact once the emotions are recognised, felt, acknowledged then accepted.

Many people feel that they are thrown into life, with no choice or control over what happens to them. While they might not be in control of the circumstances, we all have control of how we perceive and react to challenging situations. On a soul level, everything was agreed - we simply have forgotten. Remembering is helpful at any stage of grief or turmoil, and it is usually a great relief to know there is purpose to suffering. Most will endure hardship, heartbreak, loss or isolation at some stage in order to work through the correlating emotions.

What if the purpose of life is to accept situations we are presented with, allowing our soul to simply reunite as universal energy with other souls partaking in this experiment called Humanity?

I view life as a stage play, and those moments when we cry out, "This wasn't in the script!" are designed for us to blossom into a kind human who values themselves and others. We come to experience emotion, then overcome humiliation, abandonment, betrayal, rejection and equality in our personal lives. All of us have one or more of these bruises to work through.

Within what is known as the "New Age Movement" we often hear of the quest for enlightenment and unconditional love. Neither are achievable, nor are they the purpose of life. Our omnipresent soul is already enlightened and unconditional. Here we are supposed to get messy.

Life happens to challenge different parts of our being, to highlight emotion and experience the treasures a physical body is capable of, such as the magic of touch, taste, smell, sound and vision. Consider the sensation of physical pleasure or pain, consumption of food and beverage, the ecstasy of being in love, the smell of rain, the beauty of nature, the awe of procreation and the opposite as well.

Some refer to *ego* in the sense of egotistical, conceited or self-absorbed; I believe the ego is our source of willpower. I refer to the ego as free will. Life provides the opportunity to engage with the human aspect of our psyche while mastering the ability to be vulnerable with our emotions, which in turn, enhances the ability to accept what transpires. Transparency is a loving way to exist. Life is certainly not about abolishing the will, on the contrary, we need it. Willpower is the driving force of life - it is not healthy to deny or attempt to rid ourselves of it. Our will is the essence of who we are individually and our soul is energetic support while we are incarnated.

Being human ensures we have willpower. We need it, we can never get rid of it, at least not while we are incarnated, because battling our free will (ego) is the very reason we come to Earth. By discerning what is our free will (mind), then incorporating it with our barometer (body), psyche (spirit) and emotion (senses) we discover a balance between them. Reaching a happy medium of flow is how we reach contentment in life.

Emotions that we suppress or endure, ones which cripple or

elevate, are the concealed parts of us that we can choose to explore, show to others, or hide and deny with assistance from our will. Our body is a vehicle with the tools to reveal or conceal the metaphysical effects of intangible emotions. Being transparent is the ability to be vulnerable by allowing feelings to be witnessed by others. Admitting how deeply we feel affected emotionally can be the hardest challenge of all.

This book showcases how I became consciously aware of what I agreed to encounter during this incarnation. I dissect my loves, losses, and relationships, explaining how they attributed to losing my identity and regaining it. Just as Paul McCartney wrote and performed with the Beatles, it has been a long and winding road for which I have no regrets.

I am inspired to share my life with the goal that people may find peace with every choice they made and accept their shortcomings. By telling my stories in everyday terms, I present concepts as examples which can be more easily comprehended. Those who resonate with things I have done or recognise parts of me within themselves might stop beating themselves up with self-imposed guilt, living up to unattainable standards, or remaining in a stalemate because they believe others are responsible for where they are in life. Being our true self is tricky, especially given that most of us cannot comprehend what it means. Soul searching is an incredibly liberating stage that propels us forward with insightful knowledge of who we really are.

My wish is that people relate to my stories and consequently be more lenient on themselves and others, initiating an internal movement to carry on in a kinder, more positive way. None of us are victims; we are in fact volunteers who embark on our lives with the life map and capacity for potential. All the circumstances we encounter form part of our life plan, from a supportive friendship, a loving relationship, to the grief or relief of a loved one passing away, enduring abuse or experiencing an early sexual encounter. Our role in this play called "Life" is to experience as a volunteer assisting others to do the same. I explain this concept throughout the chapters.

I want us to lose the mindset that we deserve to carry guilt or to suffer for things we have or have not done and to awaken the ability to look insightfully at why we and others behave in certain ways; in doing so, we move towards acceptance, resulting in immense freedom.

Throughout this book, my life circumstances highlight how I evolved into the person that I am today, showcasing the family I chose. My deep fear of rejection, and how it transformed my self-worth. The calling to assert myself and gain courage to clearly communicate. My body image concerns and other irrational fears which were the driving force behind my passive people-pleasing persona.

Once I saw a psychic reader who told me I was lucky in love. On reflection, love did seem to fall in my lap. Well, boys were interested in me. I was blasé, rarely distracted by a boy just because he fancied me; I responded only if I felt drawn to him. Now I know why. Relationships are substantial learning devices. My love partnerships provided me the opportunity to experience love for a man with a side effect of morphing into self-imposed oppression - then gathering the courage to release myself. These relational ties manifested the perfect conditions for me to embrace my insecurities and stop living a lie by behaving out of character because of them.

I share my intense, fully reciprocated "love at first sight" soul connection and the ensuing emotional turmoil. I am certain that other souls arrive as agreed in our universal plan, despite any morals we personally uphold or human judgement we project onto them. Fated unions cannot be avoided. It is encouraging to know they present predestined opportunities to invoke change of some sort, either to spark the desire to improve, dissolve or adjust an attitude, relationship or circumstance.

These chapters highlight my progression towards intuitive work and my obsession with personal development, self-awareness and the human psyche. This transition revealed my idiosyncrasies, insecurities, incredible strengths and innate natural abilities. A path was paved, enabling me to guide and influence others to be more comfortable in their own skin, flowing on to the subsequent development of SoulLife™ Coaching. I discovered simple ways to work with the human psyche through embracing imperfections and disorders.

Most issues are nothing of the sort; they are in fact the building blocks of transformation in disguise. Challenges to our physical, mental and emotional wellbeing can be overcome by delving for the bigger picture. As we explore our character we come to appreciate diversity and discover the reason we are here.

I do not believe anyone is bad at the core, neither is any soul more or less advanced than another; we are simply here doing different things. Contrary beliefs are driven by human perspective, of hierarchy and linear time, neither of which exist in the energetic realms where we are from.

During my process I discovered how easy it is not to practice what I preach. It is infinitely easier to be on the outside looking in at someone else's circumstances and to assist them, compared to doing the same in my own life. You see, it is unacceptable to dictate to someone else how to feel or how they should react even though it is human nature to do so. We each experience our feelings uniquely, and they assist in uncovering insecurities as part of defining that process.

Looking within is a tough task, eventually surfacing as a liberating adjustment in attitude. Until then, we find it easier to believe that someone else is at fault, rather than owning the role we agreed to partake in. The reality is that the most effective person to help us is *ourselves*. When the penny drops, clarity reveals we are the catalyst for everything that happens and no one is a scapegoat.

Acceptance of perceived inadequacies is key. View each challenge as a puzzle piece providing the chance to grow into a complete jigsaw, able to expand with additional pieces at any time. Life makes sense once the purpose in any situation is exposed. The reward is personal contentment as we stop hiding behind distractions or expecting others to make us happy or feel worthwhile.

My navigation through life is far from over. Without a doubt there is a whole other phase coming, with many more experiences to enjoy or endure. These will enable me to acquire another piece that fits into the puzzle currently named Toni Reilly.

Choosing to understand rather than judge reflects a major leap in personal growth and encourages the desire to know why people behave the way that they do. Researching and observing human behaviour, while developing SoulLife™ Coaching coupled with personal soul searching, assures me that people are not as complex as I once believed. We are all weaving our way through the same few experiences designed to embrace patience, strength, courage, compassion, empathy, kindness and tolerance.

My favourite saying is: "Never say never!" - since we do not ever know what we would do until we are faced firsthand with any situation. Sometimes we need to delve deeper with an open mind, allowing the bigger picture to emerge. In order for that to take place a scene develops as a set of circumstances twist and turn, placing us in situations that cause reactions despite the morals we have been raised to believe; that is guaranteed.

I believe that we cannot comprehend any situation fully until we personally experience it for ourselves, despite being touched when someone close goes through an immoral phase, or suffers ill health, loss through death, or the breakdown of a relationship. Major life events such as the death of a loved one, a secret love affair, divorce or health crisis are catalysts to wake up, to begin the process of soul-searching, sparking the desire to know why we are here. These experiences force us into the depths of our being using grief and heartbreak as the greatest teacher. Their associated emotional symptoms ensure we emerge a wiser, more compassionate person.

My dream is that we reach a juncture where living according to our own values becomes natural, instead of adhering to outdated opinions and rules. Questioning values and beliefs instilled by family, religion, cultural expectations, commercial forces or political correctness takes courage. Adopting new values, which resonate personally, especially when they differ from what we are raised with, deserves a big pat on the back.

Join me through my transition from an ordinary to extraordinary life. Remember there are always at least two sides to every story, and if we put ourselves in other people's shoes, we begin to realise that there is good in everyone.

Collectively we can change the world; however, it is crucial that we begin with ourselves. Research what makes you tick, what ticks you off, and make peace with both aspects. One by one, as we personally shift, we create a force so powerful that it ripples out, impacting the evolution of humanity.

To experience emotions is normal.

Experiencing emotions in all their glory and force is the major purpose of life. Our soul energy does not experience them. There is no body to create self-consciousness or hide anything; we are literally transparent. In life, our body facilitates insecurities, and relationships harness love and all the feelings that go with it. The emotional rollercoaster begins when we are born and continues throughout our life. The highs and the lows, the emotions of appreciation, desperation, love, apathy and the gamut of feelings flood us. Some of us are comfortable showing emotion; others are not. For those who are not, their challenge is to be vulnerable and not allow their mind to rule over their feelings. For emotional folks, the challenge is to balance being emotional with being logical.

Life Actions

1. Do you consider yourself more emotional or more detached?

2. Do you find it easy to be vulnerable, showing openly your tears or joy?

3. Explore your emotional bruises that steer your emotional capacity.

**Connect with Toni and get
free resources to support you!**

www.ToniReillyInstitute.com/awake-bonus

CHAPTER 2:
CHOOSING YOUR PARENTS

Has the concept ever occurred to you that you selected your parents? Could you believe that your children chose you to be their parent? I believe we choose our parents and our children chose us. We pick the ones who will have particular personality traits to ensure certain circumstances, attitudes, environments and events take place in our life in order to shape us. Our parents, no matter how supportive or challenging they seem, are always perfectly aligned with the lessons we agreed to learn before our birth into the School of Life. How we grow up accompanied by the ideas which we are taught, and how our personal values and beliefs are formed, provide the key ingredients preparing us to live out our purpose. It is common for most people, at a crucial chapter in their life, to realise that these values and beliefs which are formed during childhood are not necessarily aligned with them anymore - or perhaps never were.

This realisation can occur at any stage in life. There is no set timeframe for the penny to drop. There will be many events in life that will present us with opportunities to change our approach from that of our parents to our very own.

I know that I chose my parents to raise, influence, nurture and enhance me in order to meet the predestined purpose I am here to work through. My childhood was secure and loving. I was born to extremely responsible teenage parents who were absolutely perfect for me, encouraging my free-spirited, independent personality to flourish in a nurturing, safe environment. This put me in an unrealistic state of mind as I never foresaw or expected any difficulties in life; the concept was foreign to me. I now realise that no one is exempt from harsh experiences - the ones that produce emotional turmoil, whether they present through relationships, health, loss or death. The moulding of my psyche began in childhood.

By delving into the background of your parents you can reach peace around anything that has happened. Even in cases where there is an absent parent; and, whether abusive or loving, there are small things that leave an impact on us. Discovering where our parents came from, how they were raised, and exploring their traits will explain why they behave the way they do. Just because our parents or guardians are older does not mean they know more. Our souls come together here on Earth, participating in life, to experience the challenge of lessons. Rather than remain defeated, humiliated, resentful or angry, you can free yourself of these debilitating emotions by looking hard at the psyche and history of each person to gain compassion for everyone involved. You see, when we live with resentment, we are the ones suffering the harsh emotions, not them.

I was my parent's second child, born on January 22, 1971 in Cowra, New South Wales, Australia. For the first eighteen months, Mum said I hardly slept, crying almost nonstop. I was covered in eczema, a condition where patches of skin become rough and inflamed, causing itching and bleeding. The doctor prescribed me Cortisone, which was new in the early 1970s; but Mum said she was hesitant to use it, so she applied it sparingly. That is surely her intuitive guidance, given what we know how detrimental these chemical applications can be to our health.

I have observed that some allergies, like eczema and other skin conditions are common in sensitive people, showing up predominantly in children. By sensitive I mean those who are more easily able to connect with where we are from, able to sense the energy of others with avid sixth senses. Those who are highly intuitive are able to innately connect with the universal energy. We are all capable, though for some souls their purpose may involve being some sort of messenger, alternative healer, counsellor or a nurturer of our planet and its people, animals or plants. Sensitive people are very often creative. They have a stream of connectivity to universal energy, which funnels inspiration in many forms. They become writers, musicians, actors, entertainers, speakers, or philosophers. Creativity arrives for all people as ideas and intuitive insights.

I've found that allergies seem to go hand in hand as a physical reaction to man-made chemicals found in processed food, and in other products such as soap or washing powder, which aggravate the skin of some children. It is my belief that reactions to food, fabric, grass, plants, or any substance can be attributed to being a highly intuitive child. Reactions can surface as asthma, eczema, psoriasis, dandruff or other irritable skin conditions in adults and children who are highly tuned with the intuitive energetic realms. Often they are the ones who find it harder to assimilate into the School of Life and may find it particularly challenging here on earth.

My parents were young, something I wasn't aware of until I was a teenager, when school friends would ask if Mum was my sister. Mum was seventeen and Dad was nineteen when my sister Linda was born, and eighteen months later I came along. While Mum was at home patiently taking care us, my father worked hard making a living to support the family. I've observed my mother in detail, and how her nurturing nature is different to mine. Not only that, I wanted more for my life than to raise kids or nurture a husband. I am forever thankful to her. She is the ultimate caring, kind, loving mother who sacrificed her freedom and potential to care for us.

Mum was always home. She was lovely, never cranky. She constantly let me be, which was perfect for the extremely determined, independent child that I was. I don't recall her nagging me or trying to force me to do things her way; instead, she allowed me the freedom to persist at learning to do things my own way.

If I asked for help or wanted to learn anything, she patiently showed me. My Mum taught me to tie my shoelaces and to sew and knit. Before I reached the age of ten I was cooking dinner for our family almost every night. I loved cooking and I used to experiment often. My confidence was high, riding on my ability to prepare a meal or recipe from start to finish on my own - and it certainly helped that my father always declared that whatever I presented the family with for dinner was the best meal he had ever consumed! He was consistent with praise and bestowed it on me even for my frequent disaster dinners or recipes. Practical experience was the best way for me to learn, and the bonus was: I didn't have to do the dishes. Cooking was win-win as far as I could see.

I liked helping Mum with the washing, too. I used to wash, then take the basket of clothes to hang out to dry, making me feel more mature than I actually was. Being responsible was important to me, and it came easily, as it was not expected. I wanted to do these chores, and I saw it as being trusted to carry out these grown up tasks; never controlled, as my mother let me do them my way.

My mother is my hero. She is kind, patient and loving, always there when I need her. I am thankful for how present she was when I was a child. I loved that she did not work outside the home; because of that, I've reflected on being a stay-at-home Mum myself, but concluded wholeheartedly that it would not suit me.

Occasionally Mum would drive my sister and I out to visit him in the paddock, taking him refreshments. I watched with no comprehension of how physically demanding his work was. There was no gym required for my Dad. He used these giant hooks (the kind that Captain Hook from Peter Pan has on his hand), digging them into each end of the bales of hay, then throwing each one up onto a truck until the whole tray was piled high with bales.

Life has changed so much. Body image is incredibly important to people, and manual labour is not as common. Many young people go to the gym or make time in their schedule to include physical movement to keep fit rather than being active in everyday life. For many the digital age has changed how active we need to be in our work.

Although I liked to visit my Dad in the paddock, it was a challenge as I was allergic to lucerne. My eyes always turned red and puffy while my itchy nose leaked like a tap. My nose did not stop running or itching until I reached my late teens, even though the lucerne was no longer part of our life. I was also allergic to dust mites. I had a permanent mark across my nose from pushing it up or rolling it around with my hand to stop it running or to attempt to relieve the itch on the inside of it. We needed a factory of our own for the tissues I used; they were always on hand for the hay fever I suffered, and a large pile of used ones was never far from where I was. My sensitivity haunted me with allergies, sensitive skin and eyes until I outgrew some of it in my late teens.

When I was seven, my parents took my sister and I out of school for a two-month-long road trip exploring Australia. Dad modified our vehicle, an iconic Holden Ute, by attaching a canopy that covered the back section, converting the vehicle into a van. He installed a bench seat for us to sit on for a magical adventure around our vast country. For music, Dad installed an 8-track cartridge player to listen to our collection, which was a grand total of four cartridges. We played those same cartridges so often on the trip, travelling thousands and thousands of kilometres, that it took twenty years before I was able to listen to those albums again! I love to listen to them now because of the nice memories the songs invoke.

I remember several places that we visited in greater detail than others. One is Ayres Rock, now known by its indigenous name of Uluru. My sister climbed the rock with my Dad (this was 1979, when people were allowed to climb it). Mum was pregnant with my little brother so she and I only went a short way up where we waited for them to return.

In Alice Springs we camped in a dry riverbed that filled with water in the wet season. Outback Australia is utterly amazing; the scenery and landscape were breathtaking. We travelled to Katherine Gorge, an incredible feat of nature. My favourite place was Mataranka Springs in the Northern Territory. It had natural hot springs which we swam in at every chance.

Regular school was out for the duration of our trip; instead, Mum became our teacher. She taught us our multiplication tables and we learned the time on a clock which Mum created out of a breakfast cereal box. That was the life for me! I never liked school. The girls in my class were nasty, I had no friends, and always felt isolated, lonely and left out. As life flowed for my family I attended eight different schools due to us moving around.

After nine weeks of intense driving and camping our way around Australia we returned home to Cowra. We stayed only long enough for my brother to be born and for my parents to sell our house and arrange work for Dad in Queensland. A few months later my parents packed up and moved us to Queensland to start a new life. Our family headed north, with our few possessions, on board Dad's Bedford truck with our new caravan in tow and all five of us in the cab. Mum, my sister and I sat across the bench seat alongside Dad, with the gear stick in my lap. My new baby brother lay on the floor at Mum's feet. There were no special baby restraints or legal requirements then.

I was excited to move into a caravan. It seemed like such an adventure. Dad was starting work constructing a railway line out near Blackwater in Central Queensland. When we first arrived interstate, we stayed at a caravan park. What an eye-opening experience that was! This was the beginning of a nomadic life, living in a caravan and moving around according to my father's construction contracts for the next five years. My sister Linda, brother Bruce and I had bunks down one end of our twenty-five foot-long caravan while my parents slept at the other end. There was a combined kitchen dining area in the middle with an annex, a heavy-duty canvas tent attached to the side of the caravan which sits over a cement slab to extend the living area.

We only stayed at the public caravan park long enough until the camp on-site, near Dad's project, was constructed and ready for us to move to. The construction camp was a blend of single men who were housed in portable accommodation called *dongas* and the married men lived in caravans with their families about fifty metres away.

The first night my family moved into camp, before the annex was up, Mum and Dad had put us to bed and were outside meeting all the other people. I looked out my window and saw a big white movie screen and chairs in rows outside. There was a pornographic film showing - nothing too graphic. I was seven years old and fascinated with what I saw, though I did not view much, as Mum realised that we could see out the window. She rushed in to make sure we couldn't look out. That was the only time we had the opportunity to watch, as the camp organisers reconsidered the positioning of the movie screen being so close to the families. They moved it to a more appropriate area where the single men could watch in peace.

We are sexual beings; physical touch and intimacy are a treasured pleasure granted by life in a physical body - a gift to enjoy. From a young age my curiosity was sparked by a fascination with the naked body. At that stage I had no idea that this was how babies were conceived.

Music was constant in our life. Every morning, as soon as Mum arose to prepare my Dad for work, she would turn the radio on. If the radio was not on, we played records. When I was nine,

Dad upgraded our caravan to a deluxe custom-made one, which was thirty feet long. Space was limited and we could not fit much inside, but Dad made sure we had the most important item of all: the best-sounding stereo to play our music on! My mother was a minimalist, so moving into a caravan was easy for her. We only had space for a bare minimum of things; perhaps this contributed to my detachment to material possessions.

I will never forget shopping for that stereo. For eight-year-old me, it was the most boring pastime. For months it was the priority. Whenever we drove four hours to Rockhampton to shop for groceries, necessities and supplies, my Dad researched stereos - testing them for what felt like an eternity before he made a decision, finally purchasing our stereo. After endless research in specialised stereo stores he decided on a Realistic system with a record player, double tape deck and equalizer. It was huge, sounded sensational, and was (by far) the biggest thing in our caravan. The speakers were as loud as they were large. Thirty-five years later, Dad now has his own drum kit, following his passion with music by learning to play them. There was a reason behind his intense research - he is a fantastic musician who inspired me that it's never too late to follow your dreams.

From the age of ten, we travelled by car to town every fortnight to shop for groceries. As a treat, my sister and I were allowed to buy a 45-inch single record. The best thing was being allowed to play them as loud as we liked on the family stereo. I learned from my Dad that it was acceptable to play music at extremely high volume. He led by example - he had the music playing loud when he was not at work, no matter what time of the night. I can barely comprehend how our neighbours coped; they also lived in caravans, which had very thin walls, spaced only about three metres apart! It took me a long time to realise that it was not always okay to play music as loud as I wanted to, that there were other people to consider. It goes to show, our "normal" is what we grow up with, based on what is practised and accepted in the home. Until we become influenced elsewhere, it is all we have to base our knowledge on.

My favourite camp was Oaky Creek in Central Queensland. We moved there when I was ten and left when I was twelve. It was far from town, and there was no television reception, but that never really bothered us because we preferred listening to music. The years my family spent in remote camps are memorable for me. There were lots of kids my age, so I made friends and we all went to school together. My sister started high school that year. Since there was no secondary school out in the bush, she attended boarding school in Rockhampton. I was envious; I wished I could go to boarding school, too. My envy passed as I settled into being the "eldest", more or less an only child, while my big sister was away. For the time being there was only my little two-year-old brother at home. Being there without my sister meant I took care of baby Bruce when my parents went out - and I had no one to argue with. It was bliss.

Much later in my life I realised the significance of my Dad. Growing up he was at work most of the time and not really around; I preferred it that way because he was usually grumpy and demanding of my mother's attention when he was home. It was not until my mid-thirties, when I discovered past lives and experienced my first regression, that I understood the significance of his role in my life. I recognised him (his soul) as a general in the army during the Civil War in America. Seeing him in this role reminded me of his strong opinions and views on other cultures and countries, and that he was always complimentary of the United States. In another of my past life regressions, I recognised my Dad as my husband. I was on stage in front of 120 people during a training course when I recalled that lifetime - my shock was there for everyone to witness! Fortunately I was aware and understood how souls come together here on Earth, knowing there is no incestuous weirdness in our energetic form; even still, recognising him in that role initially was strange.

Recognising my Dad in those past lives sent me into deep reflection. I recalled that when I was little I always tried to get his attention, doing little things that met with his approval so he would compliment me. My bond with Dad flourished as I marvelled at his significance and our strong connection. I was surprised to recognize how similar we are. It was a heartwarming discovery for me, as I had always thought my Dad was serious, inflexible and intolerant, when in fact, his innate nature is the opposite. Our view of our parents, compared to how friends or colleagues see them, will always differ; the interaction is not even similar, nor is it meant to be. The paradox is that a colleague of theirs may be in awe with admiration for a parent who (to you) seems distant or unapproachable.

My parents are supportive of me; they always have been. They provided what I needed by allowing me to make my own decisions about what I wanted to do with my life. I was not always thankful for their easy-going support, as it affected decisions I made around further education. It was all perfect as it turns out - this clarity only ever arrives in hindsight after we reach the understanding of how all the pieces of the puzzle fit together. Nothing happens out of context with our blueprinted path.

Once I awakened to the importance of my Dad in current life, I noticed how we interacted. I had never spent much time with him, mostly preferring to hang out with Mum, even when I visited as an adult. When I started to get to know Dad I discovered he is a great conversationalist: social, intuitive, and very much a "people person" with a lovely smiling face. I can do no wrong in his eyes - perhaps not objectively, but certainly indicative of his unwavering loyalty and favouritism which boosts my confidence. When I introduced my new work with past lives his response was, "Well, Toni, I don't understand all this, but you certainly seem passionate about it, so it must be good." What more could a girl ask for? No ridicule, only acceptance. I smile writing this, as I am in my middle forties now, and his support and interest in my work continues. Sometimes he calls to share his insight, often stating first, "I'm not psychic but..."

Mum and I are close. I always shared my experiences with her as they happened, knowing she would never scold me. If advice was warranted she might offer it, but Mum was never controlling or expecting me to do things her way. Because there was no repercussion, I was free to share all my stories through my teenage years: from boyfriends, partying, and later marriage, motherhood and a love at first sight. I never had to hide anything or distort the truth. We talked openly about life, including the ups and downs and trials. Many of our discussions formed the basis of my research into character traits, behaviours and how people interact in relationships.

I felt that I could be myself around my Mum and later my Dad, too. I believe that shaped me, instilling confidence. No matter what else was happening in my life, I knew they were there. Their support gives me the strength to continue. I know that I do not have to watch what I do or say; I never have to wonder if they are disappointed in me, or if I should call. The feeling of knowing there is no pressure, only tolerance and acceptance, is priceless. They helped form my unique beliefs. We are down to earth, everyday people.

Often (if not always) we come to learn a similar lesson as our parent or one of our parents. My main life lessons relate to rejection and equality, which at the core, relate to my self-worth, (specifically the lack of it). Likely, these challenges are similar to my mother. This means that she inadvertently showed me how to behave, as I observed her while growing up and copied what she did later in my adult life. Mum was very submissive, always nurturing my Dad. It appeared that she did whatever it took to please him, always keeping the peace while putting her own needs last. Her passive nature, dutifully taking care of the man, are the behaviours I took into my own marriage.

In hindsight, having observed the dynamic between my

parents, I have to admit that their relationship is not as cut-and -dry as it appeared to me as a child, or even until recently. Just as it is with anyone whom we are not in a relationship with, we never know what really goes on between others. Each of my parents played their role to assist in overcoming their lessons. The interaction between them becomes more and more vividly transparent to me as time goes on. Neither are victims; they are simply learning from each other.

My Dad had an unusual childhood. When he was one year old his mother was killed in a car accident in which his father was driving; she was decapitated while he sat on her lap. His father and two older brothers raised him, along with various housekeepers and carers who were not patient. My Dad grew into a very capable, responsible man who lacked the nurturing of a mother. My Mum entered his life feeling that she should make up for him growing up without a mother, even though his circumstances were not caused by her, nor was it her responsibility to make up for what happened. Mum had five siblings and easy-going parents, and she recalls a happy, carefree childhood. I believe that is why she was such an easygoing mother to me, along with her innate nurturing traits.

Looking at my choice of parents on a soul level, I am certain that they are here to support me on my journey. They are wonderful; however it is not by luck or by chance that they are my parents and I am their daughter. Their souls and mine came together as agreed: to nurture me as a unique individual when I felt secluded at school, to encourage my independence, to guide me to make my own decisions, and to assist me to develop into a person who is capable of living my purpose. My life purpose required my psyche to be prepared, confident enough, and ordinary, though flawed, to impact and influence humanity so that people might assimilate, and perhaps, alter their own perspective on life. Thank you Mum and Dad. I love you.

Even the most loving and supportive parents (adoptive or

40

biological) have a job: to deliver circumstances for our soul to learn. This means that even if they make an off-handed comparison, that is often enough to set off a core experience to help us eventually learn what we intended while incarnated. What seems like a small remark can affect confidence and cause us to develop insecurities and other issues which will have to be addressed later in life. What was done will most certainly have to be undone.

It is important to note that in our universal plan, the desired outcome of a comment or experience that has a lasting effect was supposed to imprint our psyche - to invoke emotional reactions which steer us on our set path. As life continues we remain oblivious until the assimilation is made, highlighting understanding of purpose. Clarity only ever appears in hindsight.

Accept what you cannot change.

When you observe your parents, and see them as individuals on their own quest to experience and develop in life, you begin to appreciate why they played a part in emotionally bruising you - not with vindictive intention, but for the purpose of setting you up to journey towards becoming a wiser person. Whether you felt abandoned, humiliated rejected, betrayed, smothered, neglected or loved unconditionally there lies within your feelings a challenge to overcome. Even someone who comes from a loving home will endure the reality that not everyone offers you that same security, nor are you the apple of everyone's eye, and that can be a rude awakening.

Life Actions

1. Do you want to know why you are here?

2. Are you ready to make peace with your past?

3. Begin by exploring your individual unique life map.

**Connect with Toni and get
free resources to support you!**

www.ToniReillyInstitute.com/awake-bonus

CHAPTER 3:
FRIENDSHIPS, BULLYING & SUPPORT

One of the most important aspects in life is interacting with people. After we are born, synergy begins to play out with immediate family (or, at least, with our mother). Those who navigate being adopted, never knowing one or more of their biological parents, usually are conquering the challenge of abandonment. Either way, birth is our introduction to relating to others - starting out with our parents or carers. As we grow through those formative years - the first five to eight years of life - we are introduced to other children and adults with their own individual personas. All are new to us, given our limited experience with other people so far. Our early years from birth ensure key occurrences which set us up for one or more of the challenges we agreed to encounter, ultimately forming the foundations for our purpose in life.

Our psyche will be imprinted to open avenues so we can fully experience the harshness of the emotional impact of events, depending on which bruise we are mastering to acquire wisdom, whether it is rejection, abandonment, humiliation, betrayal or equality. Later in life we have the opportunity to undertake the arduous journey of uncovering our emotional damage. In the early stages, we begin to build up resilience to allow us the strength to continue on and to live our lives each day, no matter what. We do this by creating a persona, devised by our psyche, to cover up hurt feelings and disguise these perceived flaws which rob us of our self-worth. We do this in an inadvertent attempt to shield ourselves, so that no one can see our insecurities, while we learn about enduring the impact of the bruise. It is never until we become aware of our behaviour that the process of undoing the contrived personality we developed can begin. Soul- searching takes hold to assist by guiding the way back, to embrace the unaffected innate traits we start out with as a child.

Someone navigating rejection will behave in ways that allow them to feel accepted by others, even if it is to their detriment or goes against their innate nature. One who is enduring abandonment can become dependent on others to make them feel secure and wanted.

For someone working through the bruise of humiliation, their circumstances will include scenes which create embarrassing or shameful outcomes, requiring the personality to deflect away from themselves. The art of distracting people becomes second nature: to trick them into believing they are dealing with a level-headed, confident individual rather than someone who actually feels ashamed of themselves.

Learning about the bruise of betrayal ensures the child endures an event causing them to feel betrayed (whether they were or not). To cover up this inner expectation, betrayal takes hold, creating the expectation to be let down. This child grows into an adult who becomes controlling to avoid the possibility of being betrayed by others, often doing to others what they fear most happening to themselves.

Equality produces a person who will ultimately be presented with unfair experiences and develop high expectations of themselves, all while attempting to acquire fairness for others.

To some extent all people are working through one or more of these bruises during their life, the depth of which varies in the individual. Some will have a deep bruise while others a small scratch.

It is not all challenging; each bruise works in synergy with the incredible positive, innate traits present in each of us. I believe all people are pure at the core. Usually the trauma is internal, so the harsh effects are felt most by the individual. Those around us contribute to our experience as well, to poke our bruise to unleash detrimental effects. One assurance in life is that we learn from each other by exchanging actions to create emotional responses. Each experience could be seen as a puzzle piece that we add to our jigsaw.

Life produces the means for each of us to acquire an understanding of our persona and how we portray ourselves to others. They are rarely in synergy, at least not until later in life, when our purpose diverts our attention, driving us to seek understanding of who we really are. Then we can move into the phase of unravelling the methods we developed and acted out in order to cover up the fear of being seen for who we really are at the core. We soul-search for deeper meaning to reach clarity, learning that it is okay to be vulnerable and accept life just as it is.

Those early stages of my life affected me in a deep, profoundly damaging way. Being teased from the age of four shaped me by creating a deep emotional bruise. Whenever I mentioned this phase of my life, tears of sadness erupted, right into my forties. My reaction continued until I realised the full impact of being teased. I know now I had to discover that it is okay on my own. It was necessary to develop my own ideas without the influence of peers. It moulded me to be strong enough to manage without the support of friendship and to embrace independence. I had no choice except to become okay with being outcast; my circumstances set the scene perfectly for me to grasp this challenge.

While I blossomed into an independent, unique, diverse, capable young woman with confidence in many areas, I also developed empathy and compassion for those who were different; these were the positive outcomes. The paradox is that within my relationships (especially the love ones) I became pathetically submissive. Self-effacing to avoid confrontation, I pleased to the point of putting some of my own integral needs, dreams and desires aside to reduce any risk of potential rejection from my partner. My partners were equally as unaware of this aspect of me as I was.

When I was four years old, like most children in Australia in the 1970s, I began my transition from being at home with my lovely mother to integrating into the education system. Like every other child my age I was sent off to kindergarten: a semi-structured environment for children to learn to socialise, develop fine motor skills, artistic abilities and creative talents in preparation for school. When indoors, there were puzzles to assemble, painting with fingers or brushes, and many books to browse. Each day all the children gathered around when the teacher read stories out loud. When we were outdoors there was equipment to climb, swings and a sand pit. My memories of this place are of being on my own; I did not connect with any of the other children. I daydreamed through the loneliness at kindergarten, and the best part of the day was when my mother came to take me home.

But kindergarten was bliss compared to school. In the lead-up to starting school at the age of five I was beside myself with excitement. My sister already went to school, and I wanted to be grown up like her. I could barely wait to wear a uniform. I soon discovered that learning was the easy part; socially, my dislike of segregation became amplified when (once again) I did not fit in. Nobody wanted to include me in their games. The other little girls in my class were in groups, or at least, had a friend; however, they told me that they did not want to be friends with me, because I had a "boy's name"!

I was friendless, outcast, often enduring the cruel wrath of teasing. The rejection of being excluded and disliked hurt me deeply; yet there was nothing I could do to change things. My first three years of school were spent in relative isolation, surrounded by hundreds of students to whom I was invisible. My solace came each day when I returned home to the place where I was safe and wanted.

One day in the classroom after lunch break, I was feeling sad from being rejected once again so I sat at the back behind the other students. I did not want to be seen in tears. My teacher noticed and called me to the front; she was kind, sat me on her lap and asked what was wrong. That made it worse, causing my tears to flow. I did not say anything about feeling left out, having no friends or being teased; instead, I told her I missed my Mum. At home, I never mentioned being teased to my mother either. I felt embarrassed that no one liked me, so I did not tell anyone, and I suffered in silence. I was an adult before I shared this with my Mum. At the age of five I was already covering up my feelings by lying outright about what made me upset or by omission of the true cause.

Although my classmates were nasty, I desperately wanted to fit in with them, to be a part of their group. I wanted to belong and I wished for a friend. A little voice inside convinced me that if I was called Lisa or Michelle instead of Toni, or had different coloured skin and hair, they would play with me. If only... then everything would be better. The harsh reality was that I could not change my name or my appearance - and they did not like me.

Imagine my relief when, at the age of seven, my parents took me out of school to travel around Australia for nine weeks. It was a dream - not only did I get to spend all day, every day with people who loved me, but over the course of our long trek around the country we met other families who had children my age. The two other families collectively included a grand total of nine kids of varying ages. Best part was, we all got along. Our backgrounds were different, as we were from various parts of the country; but we were united by a camping trip, being taken out of school and doing something apparently rare: exploring the vast outback of Australia.

When we returned home, my parents decided to move interstate to begin a new life. I was excited! My family was moving out of our house into a new home - a caravan - and it seemed like such an adventure to me.

When we arrived interstate, towing our new mobile home behind Dad's truck, we stayed at the local caravan park. My excitement soon deflated when we encountered other kids who lived there. My sister and I were exploring our new environment when the local children surrounded us, hurling verbal abuse. This incident united us as siblings; we had no choice except to band together and stand up for ourselves. We made a pact not to tell on each other and proceeded to yell profanities, swearing right back at the kids who were abusing us. We made a stand and it worked; the kids were not mean after we passed our initiation.

The kids living at the caravan park were only our introduction to nastiness; the ones at school surpassed them, and my school days were filled with dread. When I started at my new school I was placed into class equivalent to the level I was at in my previous school; however, when they tested me academically; I was moved up to a higher grade. From then, until I completed school, I was always a year younger than my classmates. I felt special, more grown up when interacting with these older kids, so it was good for my self-esteem..

We moved many times with the construction company Dad worked for and I attended eight schools in total, changing periodically right up until my second last year of school. I encountered varying degrees of friendship at some of those schools; unfortunately, friends for me were mostly non-existent. Given my desire to fit in, I was usually happy to change schools. It was only difficult to leave on the rare occasion where I had made a friend. I was an optimistic young girl, always believing the next school would be better.

The years my family lived in remote construction camps invoke fond memories. A Camp is a temporary community set up to accommodate workers and their families for the duration of a project. At one stage I had friends who lived at the same camp and we all went to a tiny school at Oaky Creek. The school was also temporary; classes were held in demountable buildings, allowing the whole school to be removed at conclusion of the construction project. All the primary school children were in the one classroom from grades one to seven, which equates to ages five through to twelve or thirteen. We did not have middle school. In 1982 I completed grades six and seven at that school while my sister started secondary school. Given there was no high school in the bush where we lived, she was sent to boarding school in Rockhampton, a town which was a four hour drive away

My sister only attended that school for one year. Her greatest discoveries were boys and smoking cigarettes. Boarding school never eventuated for me. By the time I was starting high school, we moved to another remote camp where I completed my first year of secondary school by distance education. Correspondence, as it was known, was the best. Each week a package arrived in the mail filled with work to be completed along with previous work marked. I usually finished my whole week's work in one day. My favourite subject was history where I learned about Greece and the pyramids in Egypt. I decided I would one day go to the see the pyramids.

In 1983, during my second year of high school at Yeppoon State High (my eighth school), my Sister and I ended up in the same year level. It was a nice change knowing someone was there for support, although now it mattered less to me whether I had friends or not. I enjoyed it there, and for the first time we both made friends who were in with the smoking crowd. I skipped classes sometimes to meet them and we smoked cigarettes and bonded. I thought I was cool - finally I was accepted, and it felt wonderful. Living in Yeppoon was nice; it was on the beach, a huge change to living remotely in the bush for me. More importantly, having friends was fulfilling. Unfortunately, it was short lived.

In 1983, Dad started a job in the coal mines, so my family moved to a town with a booming population of 1500. Glenden was a man-made purpose-built town, ninety minutes' drive west of Mackay in North Queensland. I was thirteen, and I attended high school there, starting in the middle of grade nine. The school was small and the town was in the early stages of becoming established. True to form, the first encounter at school was with some mean girls, and it was even more hideous this time. Just when I thought I had escaped separation, it started all over again. I cried at night, missing the peer group I had established in Yeppoon. This new place was loaded with bitchy teenage girls who were vocal about what they thought of the very short skirts my sister and I wore, letting us know how nice our "belts" were. In Australia we wear uniforms. Each school I attended had a different one, so initially when starting a new school, I would wear the uniform from my previous one. At thirteen, I had my fair share of body image insecurities - with the bully's bullshit compounding them. By now, I had become quite resilient to teasing and I was able to see the underlying motives behind the girls doing it. After what seemed like a long time (but was really only a couple of weeks) things began to improve, and my first special lifelong friendship was made, changing my life for the better.

Bullying and teasing excludes an individual, causing them to feel isolated. Symptoms become detrimental for the person on the end of it. The effect on self-worth is deep - more than we acknowledge. To survive, we sweep our experiences aside to get on with life, but the bruises are lasting, remaining until the time comes in our life when we are ready to explore our emotional scars. In the meantime it is human nature to inadvertently develop behaviour to cover up the emotional damage created by these types of experiences. It is important to endure these circumstances, as their purpose fosters a process for us to expand and grow.

My sister and I found a path leading through the bush on our way to school. One morning, while sitting smoking cigarettes, a girl from our new school walked by. Her name was Leanne, but I soon made a nickname which stuck, now she was known as Leebee. We discovered that she used the same track to walk to school and that she smoked as well. Right there on that dusty path our connection was made and strong friendship bonds were formed, giving my esteem an immediate upgrade.

Leebee and I are as close now as we were then. Everything is easy when I am around her. Our conversation is endless, and we still giggle like teenagers. Sometimes we cry - it depends on what is happening in our lives, but it is painless when we are together. She is a warm-hearted, kind, compassionate person who has enriched my life from the moment we met.

Fitting in with my classmates was a priority, as feeling outcast was devastatingly lonely. I wanted to be accepted, so I compromised at times just to fit in. Although I was never nasty to others, there were times when I did nothing when I saw it happening around me. This was my introduction to how negative some of the girls in the group were: being bitchy, gossiping and backstabbing each other. Their scathing comments about other students were often cruel, and this put me off two-faced behaviour for life. I decided if fitting in meant being nasty, I preferred to be alone. Finally I no longer felt as though I was on my own; now I had a friend who was sweet, too.

Being picked on demonstrated first-hand how it felt to be ostracised. There were students at school who came from dysfunctional families; the last thing they needed was to be segregated - their lives were difficult enough at home without enduring nastiness at school. Teasing people for their physical appearance made no sense to me. How could it achieve anything, except to give them a complex? Why would people do this to another person? It was not like they could change the way they were born.

As my life evolved I became aware that the girls who were nasty throughout my school years and bullies in general are just trying to fit in, too. This is a behavioural pattern to cover up insecurities within themselves. By deflecting onto others with mean taunts, they are free (if only for a moment) from their own inadequacies.

The blessing from being bullied was becoming skilled in the ability to sense what people really mean, despite saying something contradictory or deflective to take the heat off themselves or to keep them in self-denial. My work as an intuitive reader and therapist is enhanced by the empathy I feel for my clients - and I have my experiences of being outcast to thank for it. The ability to put ourselves in another person's shoes, no matter what, paves the way towards a new perspective. Whether we agree or not, it is important to accept how others view things. I personally find it extremely difficult to see people as less or more based on physical differences of race or culture. I maintain that we all experience feelings, and we all crave love and acceptance; our emotions all feel the same. We are human, no matter our background, colour or social status.

My teenage years were a lot of fun. The teasing was over and this small town nurtured a community spirit where everyone was supportive of each other. Social occasions were abundant; sometimes the whole town came together to celebrate. There were plenty of gatherings with friends to keep me fulfilled. These were the years when I became interested in boys. Even my initial relationships impacted me, as those experiences either fed my confidence or depleted my self-worth.

When I was seventeen, I moved to Mackay on the coast of North Queensland to begin an administration position at the local newspaper. My supervisor, a woman in her mid-thirties, came to the counter where I was serving customers to chastise me in front of the entire office. She told me to be quiet, and stop laughing so loud! I was so embarrassed, taking her scolding personally, that I ran to the toilet to cry behind closed doors. Being ridiculously oversensitive meant that I avoided confrontation if anyone said anything negative to me. I was seventeen and took her angry lash out to heart. I was devastated to the point of no longer wanting to work there; the oppression was too much. It turned out my bubbly, friendly personality was appreciated in another department. It took me many years to understand that not everything is about me. Even though her words cut me, she was lashing out because of how *she* felt. I later discovered that woman was unhappy with her life and with her own problems.

One evening I went with my boyfriend to meet a friend who was bringing a date, a girl from the office where he worked. Her name was Vanessa, and we immediately clicked. Had I known about synchronicity and energy then, I would have recognised instantly that Vanessa was a soul connection. This was the beginning of my second lifelong friendship; I call her Nessie.

At the time we met I lived in a two bedroom flat on my own, so Nessie moved in with me soon after. She was so much fun - always on the go, she never stopped, and she still is a ball of energy to this day. Nessie enjoyed bourbon while I smoked cigarettes and swore. In the small town where I lived the last few years, it was acceptable in conversation to swear, in fact it was as common as saying "and". I never swore in anger, though I did in conversation, simply because it added impact and became a habit. As we bonded I taught her to swear, while she taught me to enjoy bourbon. Our bond was set. We have enjoyed many fun times, and (as the universe would have it) Nessie already knew Leebee from attending a college course three years earlier when they were fifteen. So my two closest friends were already connected and the three of us have been there for each other ever since. We do not live in each other's pockets; however, we always make the effort to catch up regularly, or when each of us is in need of support. Our acceptance and tolerance of each other is beyond measure; I would say it is as close to unconditional as you can get.

All three of us have grown together from teenagers into middle age. As life goes, we were each other's bridesmaids at our weddings, we all have children, and we counsel each other whenever we need it. We have navigated boyfriends, careers, marriage break-ups and challenges with our kids. We have lost and gained weight, had health scares, and grieved at the momentous loss of loved ones. We know secrets about each other, which will always remain in the vault.

Strong friendships are a blessing when they are fuelled by choice, not obligation. The value of friendship that is loyal, objective and supportive is invaluable. Friendship is the crucial element to all good relationships - not just with friends, but with lovers, parents, and our children.

LIFE LESSON #3

Isolation creates leaders.

Isolation in childhood sets us up to be okay with thinking outside of the box. We develop the courage to state our beliefs even when they are different from the status quo. Visionary people whose mission it is to assist in the evolution of humanity will have experienced isolation in preparation to stand out, be unique or rebellious. Support may arrive through friendship, a parent, sibling, partner or mentor; but no matter who it is, their role is to lighten that feeling of separation and difference so that you feel accepted and understood enough to continue. Self-worth is the personal root obstacle resulting in hurt feelings and explains the patterns of behaviour we develop to cover up those hurt feelings.

Life Actions

1. When growing up, were you bullied?

2. Do you feel somehow different to everyone else?

3. Do you feel supported by at least one other person?

**Connect with Toni and get
free resources to support you!**

www.ToniReillyInstitute.com/awake-bonus

CHAPTER 4:
FIRST LOVE & THE
FAIRY TALE MARRIAGE

In life we are led to believe that marriage is a fairy tale, the ultimate love so spectacular and divine that together we are invincible - a union robust enough to see us through in sickness and in health. We romantisize that our soul mate or twin flame will complete us, that together we form a stronger unit than when alone. Many dream of the day they find their perfect match and live happily ever after. Hooking a husband was never my dream.

The caveman mentality instilled into the psyche of men ensures they feel pressure to provide for a wife and family, all while working hard to ensure a stable, secure home environment. The challenges for women relate to loss of identity when becoming a wife (or partner) and mother. These two aspects could be positive in other relationships; bear in mind these struggles are observed from my perspective and were underlying challenges for my relationship.

Mostly we idealise love. It is almost pointless talking about the hardships and challenges that love relationships present us with because until we have been through it ourselves we are not able to comprehend. If we were aware of hard times or the eventual messy outcome of broken relationships we might avoid the experience and that is not what life is about.

No one is ever accidently in a relationship or involved with someone that they are not meant to interact with. People may choose to believe that is the case, especially when a relationship turns sour, involves infidelity, becomes oppressive, violent, or tragedy strikes. It is quite the contrary. Turmoil of any kind is an assurance of being on path.

Our soul agrees to enter each relationship to grow. There are no exceptions, as the soul is compelled subconsciously to follow the agreed script, and the carefully planned life map quietly steers us at all times.

We select a partner who either mirrors or highlights what we have come to learn about. The relationship is not about anyone being victimised, even though it can seem that way with particularly distressing circumstances. All relationships contain a plot specifically designed to encourage growth and expansion of the human psyche. They do this by setting the scene to experience intense emotions. Love is the strongest bond to bring people together; the depth of feeling ensures a planned connection is not passed by or missed. A fated union eventuates despite disapproval, judgement or moral teachings. When the parents, family, or friends object to a union there are challenges to overcome in that relational interaction as well. If a person is here, learning to stand up for their desires, attempting to be assertive, or valuing themselves enough to take control of their own life, then circumstances will ensure family members either disapprove or do not support the couple or marriage. Depending on the lessons, the scene will be set.

When I was growing up, my mother advised me never to get married. It was her way of expressing that being married and having a husband was no fairytale - at least it had not been for her. Mum was simply sharing her view and trying in her way to save me from the same fate as her. Unfortunately this is not how life works. If only we learned from listening to advice from others! Unfortunately, that would be way too easy; we must experience relationships for ourselves. Sharing insight is great, however, as a parent or friend, the best thing you can do is accept that people (even the ones who mean the most to you) have a plan of their own, to learn for themselves firsthand. Even though Mum warned me in all sincerity that marriage was not all it was cracked up to be, when I fell in love I disregarded her recommendation. Her insights were suddenly irrelevant; I was blinded by love.

My relationship with the man I married set the scene for major development and personal expansion in this lifetime. The union and every circumstance that accompanied it enabled me to experience loving another person deeply as well as feel loved. I was set up with the perfect partner to unwittingly develop patterns of falling into behaviours to cover up my hidden, all-encompassing need for approval. I avoided any situation, which might create rejection of me at all costs. What suffered most was my identity, as I crushed my innate traits in the process.

I introduced into the relationship what I learned through my upbringing, suffering the subsequent effects. I gradually oppressed my personality by living in my relationship the only way I knew how: I copied my mother's subservient ways. She was my role model and I witnessed her behaviour, perceiving it as normal. My parent's relationship provided the representation of what I witnessed a marriage to be. My husband came with his own set of values and behaviours, formed during his upbringing, observing his parent's relationship. The stage was set, the script ensuring circumstances for me to gradually lose my identity, then find my voice in order to recover it.

When I was 13 years old my Dad invited a young man from his work to our house for Christmas lunch. His name was Rade. He was 20 years old and gorgeous, with his clear, dark olive skin, big green eyes and beautiful smile. He joined us because his family lived thousands of kilometres away, and being Orthodox, they did not celebrate Christmas until two weeks later. I felt embarrassed that Dad invited him.

He beamed charisma. He was jovial and extremely good-looking. I was not the only one who thought he was attractive; he was popular with women of all ages in our small town. Well known, not only for his good looks and friendly personality, but renowned for being involved in one incident or another - driving around town in loud V-8 vehicles, doing burnouts and other dangerous stunts. He was often the talk of the town!

I entertained a fleeting thought for about three short seconds that he might one day be my husband, a little bit odd given that dreams of marriage were not on my list of things to strive for. I made bold claims that I would never get married, believing the girls who dreamed of weddings were needy and a bit desperate. I could not comprehend the concept. Looking back now I realise that the idea of being married to him was an intuitive thought, a reminder of how my life would transpire. Eleven years later, I married him.

I had nothing to do with him after that lunch, as there was an age gap. By the time I was old enough to be more social his apprenticeship finished and he left town.

In my teens there was one boy I had a crush on, and I set out to win him. He was never interested in me, but I did not let that stop me. He became my first sexual partner. I was fifteen. That was all the liaison ever amounted to. I vowed to never allow myself to be in the situation again where I chased after someone who was not interested in me. My guard went up and there it remained.

Much later, in my forties, I became aware that this liaison set me up to shut my vulnerability down. Not being sought by this young man, I humiliated myself to get what I wanted - and all I achieved was being rejected. I intended not to allow that to happen again. This formed part of my agreed challenge to overcome rejection. He did not want me, making that fact perfectly clear. I was the one who forced my attention on him, so I facilitated being rejected by him. I felt that I was not good enough. Not pretty enough. Not thin enough. Not enough. He never said any of these things to me and none of them are really true but they are an accurate insight into my thoughts, an example of how my self-esteem took a hit. Over time, I naturally moved on. The whole experience became a distant memory; forgotten, once the required damage had been done. My psyche was moulded to learn about rejection. Another piece of the puzzle was added.

When I was still fifteen I started dating a boy who was eighteen. We were a couple for four and a half years. My initial crush passed after about twelve months together but I did not end it. I justified that it would not be nice to hurt someone who loved me. We moved in together when I was seventeen because many of my friends were living with their boyfriends and I wanted to fit in. My saving grace was starting a job at the newspaper in Mackay, a larger town ninety minutes' drive from where I lived. I moved into a flat and my desire for independence accelerated. My boyfriend worked at the mines, travelling to visit me on his days off. The rest of the time I was on my own, feeling free. After four and a half years together I gathered the courage to tell him that I was ending our relationship. I only finished then because someone else had caught my eye, and being disloyal or unfaithful was not an option. I justified that now I had a valid reason to end the relationship. The doctrine of being faithful was strongly instilled in me. For that reason I left to avoid being judged as unfaithful instead of leaving for the honest reason that I was no longer in love.

Despite no longer having strong feelings for him I did not see that as a reason to hurt him. I hurt myself instead by living in a friendly relationship; and I ripped him off too, as he could have been available sooner for his true love to come along. I did not value myself enough to leave the relationship when the spark had gone.

At nineteen I was single. What a relief, I enjoyed the freedom immensely, it was only eight months before I was back in a committed relationship. I was destined to be paired up - besides, I liked the security of knowing that someone loved me. It made me feel worthwhile.

Relative singleness was soon over when out of the blue one Saturday night my sister and I were out dancing when we ran into the young man who came for Christmas lunch when I was thirteen. He was gorgeous, and was talking to me! He was visiting for a wedding and his date had returned to their hotel. We hung out all night, and when he left, he was adamant that he would return his date home, as she was not for him. Our sixteen years together were underway.

I liked him, we talked for hours, it was easy being around him, and I felt comfortable in every way. I was impressed by his openness when we talked. He shared details about himself and secrets which I felt privileged to know. I appreciate people being honest with me. Conversing easily about some things remained throughout our marriage, and I valued that trust beyond being protected from the truth. Conversing about deep feelings, on the other hand, was not easy.

Honesty is high on my list of values. I am a liberal thinker, so not much surprised me, or if it did I would usually adjust, refraining from judging, preferring to understand when anyone shared their inner secrets or feelings with me. I prefer to know the truth even if it hurt; otherwise I feel like a fool. Later in my life I was challenged with being dished up what I gave out. I found it sad when I arrived at the harsh realisation that what frustrated me the most I did to someone else. I proved that I was not able to comply with my expectations of others and kept certain actions of mine to myself rather than risk judgement.

My future husband worked as a contract boilermaker in remote locations, usually a long distance from where I lived. There were no mobile phones then, and when he rang me from a pay phone we talked for hours. We spent all of his days off together. He was masculine, kind, warm-hearted and especially lovely to me. I felt connected to this man, and when we cuddled it was as though I could not get close enough. I was in love. We were in love.

I assumed he was the life of the party as he accompanied me on many social outings in our early dating months, always interacting with people in a friendly manner. It turned out that he was quite the opposite: introverted, preferring my company over anyone else.

Early on, without ever realizing, I began to oppress myself. This happened by holding back my opinion. I took off-handed comments personally, which eventually took its toll; and rather than feel judged, I shut down.

We went away for a weekend in our early days together, which was when I first experienced tension. It showed up in the form of the silent treatment and became regular torture in our marriage. This passive-aggressive behaviour remained through-out, and was ultimately the downfall which ended our sixteen years together. The first time it happened, we were out seeing a movie. I made a comment and I noticed he became silent. I could feel there was a major shift in his mood as he withdrew. I asked what was wrong. I asked what I had said. His answer was, "Nothing." And we spent the rest of the evening in silence. I was devastated, certain our evening was ruined because of me. When we returned to the hotel, I was in tears trying to find out what caused him to withdraw. I didn't get an answer, only an apology. No resolution. I had no idea what triggered his withdrawal but I was well aware that it happened right after I said something. In my mind, sharing my opinion caused the silence. So, I made it about me, wondering what I had done, and never realising that this was something he was dealing with that I did not understand.

After four years together, when I was twenty-four, we decided to get married. There was no romantic proposition; I was not much of a romantic. The two of us were out shopping for groceries one evening and walked past a jewellery store. I saw an engagement ring that I really liked; right then we decided to get married. He paid for the ring and, outside the jewellery store, asked me to marry him. Our wedding happened four months later.

My Dad was a little offended that he was not consulted - but it all happened so fast. There was no time to consider anyone else, we were too caught up in our bubble. We were getting married!

Here is where my life became contradictory; my actions did not represent my views or beliefs. The last thing I dreamed of was getting married. I felt that marriage was relinquishing independence and wondered why anyone would want to do that. My opinions did not stop me becoming swept up in the euphoria of someone wanting to spend their life with me – plus, I wanted to commit to this man because I was in love. I certainly never envisaged a traditional religious ceremony, as I was not religious. My sentiments about religion were steadfast by this stage, strongly influenced by my Mum, coupled with a comment made to me by a priest visiting my primary school for a religious education lesson.

Mum warned me for as long as I can remember, "Don't get married Toni!" I understood why she gave me this advice, given that she married young and it proved to be no fairytale. I was convinced that it was different for us. I was blinded by love. Despite her lifelong advice, Mum was supportive of my decision.

Confrontation with organised religion emerged when I was eleven years old. A priest visited my school to teach religious education. When I mentioned to him that my Mother was not christened (baptised) he took me aside after class with great concern and kindly advised me to talk her into getting christened – otherwise, she would go to hell. I was distraught. I loved my Mum more than anyone. I could not bear the thought of anything bad happening to her. What was hell anyway? I had no idea, but it sounded frightening. I went home from school that day hysterical inside. I told her what the priest said and asked her to get christened. She explained that this was not true and assured me there was nothing to worry about. Mum shared that she did not believe in religion, mainly because her father had warned her as a child to be especially wary of priests.

Given the outrageous power that priest held over me, I wondered what happened to my Pop, for him to be so adamant to warn his children not to get involved with the church. Mum and I have spoken about Pop's choices around religion and she does not know what caused her father to have such distaste for it. We assumed he may have been mistreated or sexually abused but that has never been confirmed. Now my Poppy has passed so I cannot ask him, at least not in person.

Mum's assurance did nothing to put my mind at ease. For months I lay awake at night worrying that she would go to hell. That experience instilled dread in me; for something I had absolutely no control over, though it did eventually cause me to question religion. After much reflection at the age of eleven I concluded that it could not possibly be right to instil fear into a child in this manner. Even if there were a God, this representative went against the principles of being a good person. I doubted from then, and over the next couple of years determined my overall outlook on organised religion. While I believe the foundations of religions are virtuous it seemed to me that people have to live up to a strict ideal to be considered good enough. I deemed myself to be a good person - maybe not *their* kind of good, but I am kind and compassionate. I gave myself a tick of approval with assurance from my heart that kindness was the most important characteristic in people.

Despite my aversion to religion and church I remained true to my passive nature of keeping everything smooth, avoiding disharmony at all costs. I went with the flow for our wedding plans. I was not interested in a church wedding, as I was not getting married for cultural or religious beliefs, nor for the ceremony or to wear a white dress; I simply wanted to be committed to this man. My husband's mother was religious and her wishes were met with us having a church wedding. In her culture a wedding is an important event for family, friends and their community. My inability to speak up meant I was married in a church, dressed in white.

I did not like being in the spotlight, and in the lead-up to the wedding I had a meltdown. I felt overwhelmed because the list of guests kept growing – meaning, I would be standing up in front of all these people. My feelings were irrelevant, as his Mum was concerned with tradition and what the people at church thought. This wedding was an important opportunity to showcase how proud she was of her son.

We were married on May 6, 1995 at the Serbian Orthodox Church on Vulture Street in South Brisbane. The ceremony was a shock to me in a few ways. We lived in a small town, twelve hours' drive from where his parents lived, so we rarely saw them. I was aware that his parents were Serbian, but I had no idea what that meant as far as culture went. I was uncultured, being raised in small towns and remote areas, and I had little understanding of any foreign culture. I only knew what little I learned in history class in the first year of high school, which was geographically and historically oriented.

I had visited Brisbane a few times as my friend lived there. I had to organise the wedding from Mackay, twelve hundred kilometres away, before the Internet; so this process was tricky logistically, coupled with my non-existent experience at organising events and a carefree attitude to details like flowers, catering, venues, musicians and all the other things that go with organising a wedding! My sister-in-law, whom I had only met once or twice, came to the rescue. She was a godsend, taking over the arrangements while checking in with us on details and preferences.

She was the most engaging person I had ever encountered. I could hardly believe my luck. I was in awe that I would soon be related to her. She was clever, warm, stylish, teaching me about personal style, introducing me to coffee, appreciation of fine food and wine. She initiated me to wonders of the city: art, buildings and other objects that I had never considered relevant, let alone exquisite. She used to say, "I wish you were my sister when I was growing up." Another synchronistic important soul connection had entered my life.

Our wedding went ahead with one hundred and fifty guests. The ceremony was in Serbian, a foreign language to me. I joked that the priest could be saying that my new husband could do as he wished with me - and he may have been, because I could not understand a word. I did not stand up for my wishes, so I was not represented in the ceremony. I silenced my personality and put aside how I wanted my wedding, and it went ahead without much input from me. It was a sign of how things would turn out.

Being a sideline in a ceremony where I was not really represented was strange. I was not used to being dictated to, as my parents allowed me to make my own choices. They guided and instilled goodness and were there to support me. I did express my personality with my bridesmaids; I wanted them to wear short suits, but they were not keen. We compromised and they wore skirt suits instead.

I had no attachment to the content of the ceremony, at least from a religious perspective. I went along with it anyway. In hindsight I was a coward, unable to muster the courage to stand up for what I believed, setting the scene for my demise within my marriage. After the ceremony, all the guests (most of whom I did not know) congratulated me. They kissed me on the cheek three times - my introduction to Serbian culture! Despite the incredible culture shock, the thing that bothered me most was, during the ceremony, they tied our hands together, crowning us King and Queen, and it ruined my hair.

I have since developed into a much more romantic person, and in retrospect I can fully appreciate the beauty and cultural tradition in my wedding ceremony.

At the reception I was stunned when my new husband made his wedding speech. He did not make one, he made two; first he spoke in English, followed by fluent Serbian. I was completely unaware that he spoke another language. Even though I was impressed in that moment, after four years together it dawned on me how little I knew of my new husband's culture or his upbringing. It was something he avoided talking about.

I discovered he had a strict childhood, which explained why he moved to a town so far away from his family when he joined the workforce. He was attempting to be a good son at the expense of his own freedom.

When my turn came to make a speech I could not. An intense fear of public speaking meant I lost my voice, literally. I was not able to make a speech (and my social interaction was limited as well) but I still enjoyed our reception. My family and friends were there, ensuring a fun time, even though I was barely audible.

People believe we lose our voice because we are ill, however loss of voice metaphysically relates to not being *heard*: a need to speak up for ourselves, or say what we really mean, how we feel in any situation. The body reacts physically, which is our soul's way of asking us to look at what is happening in our life at the time that any physical reaction occurs. For me, not voicing my desires created my loss of voice. My husband knew what they were, but he was also not in charge of our arrangements. I could not get through to his mother, as she had her hopes and dreams for her son's wedding. Losing my voice was a sign for not stating my views and desires for our wedding day. If only I realised from a higher perspective then, things may have been different. It took another ten years to begin stating my opinions to him.

A couple of days after our wedding we flew to the United States for our honeymoon. It was my first time travelling out of Australia. We had four months off work and a vague plan for exploring the USA. We landed in Los Angeles. During the day I found it hard to stay awake, which was my body clock adjusting to the time zone difference. Little did I know that international travel would become a major part of my future.

We rented a car at times, and given that I was twenty four and you had to be twenty six to get an international license, my husband did all of the driving. I was happy about that as driving on the opposite side of the road was a challenge I did not feel the need to face. Luckily I was not behind the wheel because I fell asleep a lot on the long road trip across America. My husband wanted to fit in as much sightseeing as possible, so we were in the car often, stopping off to check out museums and landmarks, always quickly moving on to the next place.

I craved to stay somewhere long enough to meet people. I love conversation, listening and learning from people is my style, rather than reading history in a museum. How we live now is more interesting to me than how they lived then. Our honeymoon was a never-ending trek, stopping for as short a time as possible before hitting the road again, bound for the next town or city.

We were on a budget, which meant sometimes we slept in our hire car when we had one. We saw lot of the USA, travelling from the West to East Coast. My favourite cities were San Francisco, New York and Boston. I dreamed about living in Manhattan. I wished we could stay, living like the natives, at least for a few months. I adored the hustle and bustle during our five days there; it was the longest we stayed in one place. I wanted to go out to bars and restaurants to engage in conversation with the locals – plus, I was curious to see all aspects of New York City. Exploring how people really live is my favourite activity, but my husband was different; he was on the move, eager to make it to the next place. Being happy with my companionship, he did not need other people to talk to. In fairness to him, I never told him what I wanted to do. I went along with everything he suggested.

Again, submissive - not because anyone disagreed with me, simply because I opted not to share my desires and opinions. Why not? I did not want to risk the silent treatment. If I kept quiet, I would not risk stressing him. I was already pathetic in my attempt to avoid feeling rejected. I made excuses about not upsetting my husband, but really, I was submissive so that I never ran the risk of being judged by him as high maintenance. I behaved this way to my own detriment to avoid confronting my worst fear of not being liked.

His dream was to drive around America. The fact that he loved cars and driving was no secret to me. It was not until we had been travelling for a few weeks that I became acutely aware of how different our personalities and traits were. He was introvert; I am mostly extrovert. This realisation was a surprise to me. I pondered what it meant, though I never shared my observations with him, fearing I might hurt his feelings.

At this stage I became slightly aware of my inability to say what I felt or meant, or to say what I wanted. I was not yet aware that my passiveness stemmed from avoiding any interaction that might leave me feeling rejected. My inability to be honest with my partner and myself took hold as I became almost fully incapable of being assertive. My tendencies were brought to my attention, though I did not take notice.

The concept that I was being myself never entered my realm of thought at that stage; in fact, it was at least eight more years until I faced up. I ignored how important relating with people was to me, how much I thrived on interaction with others. One on one with my partner, as much as I tried, was never going to fulfil me entirely. I needed other people in my life as well.

Relationships are our teachers.

Every interaction with another person is an opportunity for each to learn from the other, not to be the victim of the other. You come together to grow and explore emotions together. No matter the circumstances between the two people, ceremony - whether inspired, or dictated by religion - is in our life to develop a sense of self. Our ability to question doctrines and man-made morals is a liberating gift but is challenging to acquire. Going against the grain of what everyone else is doing takes courage.

Life Actions

1. Have you ever been in love?

2. Were you really in love, or were you escaping from overbearing parents, getting out of an unstable environment, or seeking practical security?

3. Did the other person feel the same about you, or were they trying to escape something else, too?

**Connect with Toni and get
free resources to support you!**

www.ToniReillyInstitute.com/awake-bonus

CHAPTER 5:
FAMILY AFFECTS MOTHERHOOD

Creating a family is a magical thing, an intrinsic part of my evolution. I discovered firsthand that giving birth and raising children is no fairy tale. Adorable and sweet as they are, children are born with a distinct personality of their own. Contrary to the occasional outspoken person who may not have had children or who did not find parenting challenging, not everything children do is a result of the parents or lack of parenting skills. Individually we arrive in this world with a life plan, including a need for love, along with our predetermined personality. All traits are in perfect alignment to see us through our soul plan and to overcome certain challenges and experiences during incarnation at the School of Life. Tricky traits such as "determination" are part of our psyche from the moment children are born, and while this trait is incredible for driving a person to compete and prosper in the face of resistance, it can pose a challenge for parents and carers when the child does not adhere to the rules or expectations of how a child should or should not behave.

The only way a tiny baby can communicate that something is wrong, or they have a need, is to cry. If we are not tuned enough to know what they want then we are guaranteed to have some distress as a mother or father attempting to comfort our child.

My parental instincts kicked in immediately. Ensuring my child was peaceful and comfortable was paramount for both my baby and my sanity. Love bonds ensure that our children survive, as the trying times can be so demanding it could potentially drive people to behave out of character or try one's patience to their limit. For some new parents there is loss of sleep. The effects cannot be assumed; in order to comprehend sleeplessness, it has to be felt. Sleep deprivation has been used to torture people, so it should not be dismissed offhandedly! I have heard people scoff at the whining of parents discussing their lack of sleep - those parents who have not experienced a child who did not sleep well, or was demanding, will not know what it is like.

Just like all other scenes in one's life play, parenting is part of the plan for some, while not for others.

Childbirth was an incredible experience for me. The inexplicable bonds between Mother and Child are a treasure in my life. Becoming a mother was not all rosy. The physical pain of childbirth is something I had not heard much discussion about, and I guess it is one of those lightly spoken areas that remain somewhat a secret until it happens. After giving birth, when cradling each newborn bundle, love or shock took over and the pain was forgotten, until the pain of delivering the afterbirth takes over to reduce the uterus to its pre-pregnancy state. While learning to breastfeed my first baby, cramp-like pains kicked in; and with each subsequent delivery the afterbirth pains increased. I gave birth three times and pondered the extraordinary pain threshold of women who have given birth more times, considering only the initial physical pain in the weeks following delivery - not the lifelong challenges of family interaction.

One thing is absolute. There are two distinct phases: life before children and life after – and the two are in no way similar. The impact of a baby who is dependent on you for everything is incredible, amazing, challenging and unexpected. Of course life adjusts quickly, with these memories slipping into the background of what can seem another lifetime.

You might think that some of this information would put us off having children, although it does not. We are here to procreate. Our memory is short, or we become disillusioned, or we build up a fantastic dream which differs from the reality.

When Rade and I returned home from our honeymoon we agreed to start a family of our own and were successful immediately. I was pregnant the first month we tried. I was excited, flattered that this man wanted to have children with me.

It never occurred to me at the time that I believed it was the only option for me. I thought that having a family was what you did once you were married, was it not? Since the man I married liked children and was happy about having a family of his own, I dreamed of how lovely it would be to have a large family. I told people that we were planning to have six children. I had no idea what it was like to be a mother and was actually excited to please, as Rade loved kids and the concept of family. Prior to marriage, I had no desire to have children and was happy working and being free of responsibility.

Being pregnant was physically a shock (at least initially). From the day of my positive pregnancy test at four weeks along, I struggled to stay awake. I could barely keep my eyes open and that tired feeling lasted until I reached 12 weeks. The rest of my pregnancy was smooth sailing.

I decided to continue working as close to my due date as possible because at that time I had no intention of returning to work. We planned for me to be a stay-at-home mum, taking care of our children. That is what my Mum did, so it is what I agreed to do. As with many things in life, the reality was different to my theory, and the way that I envisioned being a mum who stayed at home taking care of her children would be different as well.

I finished work a week before I was due, and at 4 a.m. on the 19th July 1996 (one day after my due date) I woke with labour pains. I knew to time the intervals between the pains and they came every five minutes, right from the first one. Rade drove me to the hospital and our lives were about to change forever.

During my first pregnancy I dreamed that I was having a baby girl with dark hair. We did not find out the sex, as I wanted it to be a surprise. Labour was unforgiving - painful like nothing I had encountered, and when I was close to being fully dilated the labour pains were excruciating. I was afraid to have an epidural and chose to only have gas for pain relief. The nurse gave me Pethidine, which was awful; all it did was make me feel sleepy until I was forced wide awake with the next excruciating labour pain. With one hand I held onto the gas mask for dear life, working through the pain; and with the other I squeezed Rade's hand so tight his circulation must have almost cut off. I vomited at some point and the midwife announced I was 8.5 cm dilated. Soon after my baby girl was born, naturally. We named her Bebe.

Not long after meeting my baby, she was taken from me and put into a crib while my perineal tear was stitched up. When my parents arrived I was still in the labour suite, and they came over thinking I was about to have the baby; they were surprised when I pointed over to the crib where Bebe was sleeping. They were grandparents for the first time.

I was still in a state of shock when I came out of the labour ward to return to my room. On the way I noticed other women who had not yet given birth. I wanted to let them know how painful it was; I wanted to ask if this was their first time and did they know how much it hurt, but that would be ridiculous and pointless. There was no turning back. Just like me, they had to give birth. I expected having a baby would hurt, assuming the pain was from the baby making its way out of the pelvis, stretching and expanding to accommodate the head. That did hurt, but only a fraction compared to the intense labour pains whose purpose is to open the birth canal up. Well, I knew now! I was relieved that my baby was out.

Bebe looked around as if she was taking everything in, and the nurse said "she's been here before." The concept of reincarnation had never entered my mind until then, but the look in her eyes suggested that she was back again. I watched her eyes while she studied me and her surroundings.

My first and only night in hospital had me pacing the hallway to stop Bebe crying. The nurse offered to take her so I could get some rest, but I could not rest. I was wired knowing that no one could take care of my baby as well as me. When I cradled her she would be quiet. Interestingly, right up to the day before giving birth, the sound of crying children annoyed me; now, when my own child cried, all I wanted to do was soothe her to make her peaceful.

Now I was responsible for a beautiful healthy daughter and I bonded immediately with her. Rade was delighted, asking to have us at home as soon as possible, so at his request I left the hospital twenty-four hours after giving birth - with no real idea of what to do. I left the hospital feeling confident that I could care for my newborn. I hit the ground running. There was simply no other option. Bebe did not feed well and she screamed most of the time unless I was cradling her. The first night home was weird. I had this person who relied on me twenty-four hours a day, and I thought to myself, "What have I done?" The reality that life would never ever be the same began to sink in. I had many questions running through my mind, the strongest being: "What am I supposed to do with her?"

I planned to breastfeed, as I was told that was best for babies, and my body kindly provided me with breasts. Bebe cried all the time, though I always felt calm, never annoyed or impatient. I attempted to breastfeed with little success. After a few weeks of her constant crying I changed to a bottle and she began to gain weight. The side effect of infant milk formula was wind, which causes nausea and reflux, and she cried. Man-made nutrition did not agree with her little system and she vomited all the time.

My life was different to such an extent that there was nothing I could do without this little person. My baby needed loads of cuddles, she never outgrew hugs. I carried her most of the time, as she would not go to anyone else, only me or her Dad.

Rade was a caring father, patient and loving. As soon as he returned from work, the first thing he did was cuddle Bebe and play with her; but he was far from modern, leaving everything practical up to me. I set those boundaries for how the family ran in our house, with me attending to all the practical needs of our baby and the home. I carried out the domestic chores, changed all the nappies and cooked the meals. It was not something I dwelled on. I was in the mode, operating on autopilot, like clockwork.

When Bebe was 15 months old I gave birth to my second child, a beautiful little boy that we named Reo. Something strange happened in the birth suite. Reo was born soon after I arrived at the hospital, and I distinctly recall that the moment he entered this world, something switched in me. It was strange, as though at that moment my mind went flat. I do not know how else to describe it. I felt flat, my vibrant personality vanished, and I had just been handed my treasured little boy - the dream of many, to have a pigeon pair of children.

I left hospital with my new son in less than twenty-four hours, as my Mum was taking care of Bebe. Returning home with a newborn the second time was different. I knew how to care for a baby, and my baby boy was feeding easily; he did not cry all the time like his sister had. On the day I arrived home with Reo, after a short time, my Mum left and my husband returned to work. I guess they assumed I was an old hand. I felt weird, and as soon as I was alone I burst into tears. I stood crying in the lounge room with my twenty-four-hour-old son in his crib and my 15-month-old daughter playing on the lounge room floor. I did not know why, so I coped, never mentioning my outburst or feelings to my husband. For some reason I thought that I was exempt from the baby blues and never made the assimilation, or associated my lack of emotion, feeling flat all the time, with postnatal depression.

Reo was eight months old when I snapped back to my usual vibrant self. I had been in this bizarre blur where I functioned doing all that was required of me, minus my natural enthusiasm. I was usually a cheery person; I lost it, only realising the extent of the low when my usual self reappeared. Returning to myself was the best feeling I can describe. I was back, without consciously realising I had been gone. That is when I knew I had been through postnatal depression.

My son was an adorable, low-maintenance baby who smiled and laughed all the time. He used to wake in the night to feed. When he was 8 months old the fun began, training this strong-willed little man to sleep through the night.

During my stagnant personality period we moved from Mackay to Brisbane to start a new life. I wanted to move to the city. Bigger was better. However, I had not anticipated the adjustment of being away from my friends and family. I was somewhat detached from my friends at that time, as I was the first to start a family, and taking care of them took almost every moment to maintain a routine to ensure my sanity remained intact. Within a couple of weeks of having Reo, my best friend Ness gave birth to her first child, so we occasionally spent time together during the day. That all changed when we moved and I adapted to living with Rade's parents at their home in Brisbane until we found a house of our own.

About the time we moved in with Rade's parents in Brisbane, his mother had a stroke and underwent major surgery to fix her arteries, which turned out very well. That was busy, and I nursed her back to health while I took care of my two babies. My mother-in-law took a little effort as she was not used to being nursed, but when she recovered she was a great help to me. She minded one or both of the babies while I escaped to the shops occasionally. That free time meant the world.

Around this time all the adults in the house became ill with a virus so debilitating it was almost impossible to get out of bed. I wished I was dead. Dramatic, I know; but I had been ill for some time, unable to move, with every part of me aching. Then my fever returned with vengeance as my illness developed into pneumonia.

Metaphysically, pneumonia indicates an unexpected event that impacts personal space. Health issues with the lungs are an indication of underlying sadness and feeling suffocated by someone or a situation. This physical manifestation was my body's way of telling me that I needed my own space - probably time out from being a Mum as well as living with my parents-in-law. I did not realise this at the time, as I always behaved in a way that ensured no one was upset by my wishes. These health issues all fit with what was happening in my life then, but I was still unaware - living life day by day, taking care of my responsibilities as a mother and wife, that *Toni* was lost, somewhere in the distant background. I had been invisible for some time, without me realizing. My identity had gone into deep hibernation and I was only twenty-eight years old.

We found a house close to the city, and that is where Rade and I moved into with Bebe and Reo. There was a girl who lived two doors down who befriended me. That interaction was a godsend, as I was on my own there, in the city, at home, taking care of two small children while my husband worked. I was able to get my kids into child care one day a week for a break. On that day, for stimulation, I went to work at the Credit Union where my friend Leebee worked. It was bliss to get dressed and leave the house. I felt like a real person for those few hours when I was at work.

Even though we moved close to the city, weekends were spent out at my in-laws' place. They wanted to see the children, and Rade had friends out there whom he liked to visit. He loved showing his family off, so we went in the car driving around almost every weekend.

When I was 28 I went with my two best friends for my first psychic reading. I was excited to have some time out. We had our readings and went for lunch. That reading was pivotal for me. It awakened me to my oppressed state and how I had slipped into it. I became acutely aware that my characteristics were different to my young children. I actively attempted to avoid hurting their precious feelings by understanding our differences and being mindful of my behaviour that could potentially impact them.

Day-to-day I was content. Life was ruled by the routine of caring for my young children and their father when he returned from work. Cooking, shopping for groceries, gardening, cleaning the house, washing, along with all the usual chores that go with running a home and family.

During another moment of planned madness, I fell pregnant for the third time. Working outside of the home just one day a week was my saving grace, and I worked until I was due to have my third baby. Not long before I gave birth for the third time, we moved again, this time a few suburbs away into a bigger house to accommodate our growing family. At 28 years of age I was the mother of three children under four years old. Giving birth to three planned babies in three and a half years meant my life became a blur. My day started around 4 or 5 a.m. when the first child woke up.

Coco, my youngest, was peaceful and did not cry much at all. When she was a few months old, like me, she developed eczema all over her precious skin. This is where my introduction to natural remedies began, as I was not keen to treat her delicate skin with cortisone. I delved into Chinese medicine in an attempt to cure her. Acupuncture and changing to PH balanced soap and liquid washing detergent cleared it up.

As mentioned previously, I believe that eczema, is a side effect of children and adults who are sensitive. I have observed that those with these types of skin conditions have a heightened sixth sense. Also, to a certain extent, they do not cope well with man-made products and food additives. Their physical system is as sensitive as their sixth senses.

By the birth of my third child, I was unperturbed, and felt able to deal with whatever might happen. As it turned out Coco was the easiest baby of all. Perhaps because I felt calm with being a Mother, and knew what to do or perhaps I was allowed a smoother experience. Coco slept through, she barely cried and was content all the time. Even still, I decided there would be no more babies for me.

I love and adore my three little children. I studied them, their interaction together and how their individual personalities were different to each other and to me. I wondered about what it would be like to interact with them when they became teenagers and adults. Something inside of me knew that Motherhood was not the only important aspect to my life.

Parenting theory does not reflect reality.

Parenting small children is relentless, and each person will experience being a mother or father in their own way. Motherhood proves that theory does not accurately reflect reality. Natural does not mean easy. Giving birth is an example of learning tolerance by accepting other people's experiences even when you cannot put yourself in their shoes. It is important that we own our experience; adjusting details or omitting feelings to fit in with anyone else's expectation is lying to ourselves.

Life Actions

1. Think about a situation where someone showed you tolerance even though there was no way of them knowing what it felt like to you.

2. Can you think of a time when you showed tolerance?

3. Is tolerance a normal experience for you?

**Connect with Toni and get
free resources to support you!**

www.ToniReillyInstitute.com/awake-bonus

CHAPTER 6:
THERE HAS TO BE MORE

My compulsion to observe the function of human nature, discerning which traits are innate and which are learned, lead to understanding my own behavioural patterns and how they affected other people. My inner process shed light and opened a wormhole towards uncovering my philosophy for why we are here.

This chapter showcases the beginning of my awakening, when I became aware that there was more to my life. This insight gradually increased deeper into my psyche than I ever imagined. My purpose had been playing out my entire life, even though I was oblivious. This is the story of beginning to realise my innate wisdom and the discovery that we are all wise, each here blended with an incredible energetic eternal force; that is, our soul. Each and every life is planned out like stage play, with meticulously detailed and concise forethought, orchestrated to ensure we learn as intended while we attend the School of Life.

At some stage we will be made aware that there is more to our existence than the physical body housing our soul. Leading to the discovery that each of us has our very own infinite, all-knowing library of wisdom, so powerfully precise, which we can call upon for answers, guidance and affirmation during our incarnation.

When I was 28 years of age, and while I did not know it at the time, this age heralds a significant astrological time in people's lives; it is known as a "Saturn Return." This influence represents and conjures a major period of awakening for any individual, where we come face to face with the challenges our soul incarnated to overcome. It marks the beginning of a time in our lives where we enter a new phase, manifesting as the perfect circumstances to ensure we develop a new perspective around our values and what we believe about ourselves.

It was during this influence that I had gone for my first psychic reading. It delivered a planned effect, ensuring a deeply profound experience which propelled me inexplicably towards a personal awakening. Although my session was for an hour, I recall clearly only a few things the reader said. She asked my star sign (Aquarius), and my husband's (Scorpio), then remarked, "That sign squashes yours." Her comments stayed with me, ringing in my ears, causing me to examine and analyse how I interacted with Rade. I was smacked with the truth and extent of how oppressed I felt, blaring at me as I became, for the first time, consciously aware of my extreme passive nature. I faced up to the scope of which I struggled to speak up or express even the simplest things that I desired, knew, or believed in. I guess I was a people pleaser. I was fast realising that I chose to always be accommodating, opting to say nothing just in case I made waves and bought on a silent episode, or god forbid, I was challenged for my thoughts and potentially judged negatively or rejected.

By keeping my thoughts to myself I kept my feelings and opinions hidden. Disguised by my calm exterior, the unreleased tension festered around in my very busy mind with no outlet. I did not allow my thoughts the voice they desperately required; instead I repressed them in my everyday life at home with my husband and children.

Logically, it was clear to me that I caused my own suppression; I allowed it all to transpire, lacking the courage to deal with any form of disagreement. I felt as though my soul was squashed at the core. I gradually went from being carefree and outspoken to a wallflower, so much so that the transformation went unnoticed by me. I efficiently navigated each day taking no notice of my feelings. I was preoccupied with chores, work, and the practical side of life, being far too busy to take time for reflection.

There is only so long that we can hide from ourselves. I had reached a point where I was screaming inside, wanting to be acknowledged. Rather than talking and expressing my inner turmoil, true to form, I said nothing. Instead, I cried on the couch at night. That was my release - though certainly not a solution. The solution would have been simple: express my thoughts, my needs, my frustrations. I could not do it.

That psychic reader described the personalities of each of my three children (who were all under four at the time) so I was not fully aware of all of their traits, though some she noted were already evident. She explained that they were opposing star signs to mine. I am an air sign, Aquarius. My eldest daughter is Cancer. My son and youngest daughter are both Scorpio, the same as their Father.

The reader explained how detrimental it would be to call my eldest daughter names. Although I wondered who would do that to a child (or anyone), I still did not want to risk affecting any of my kids negatively. She pointed out how different their character traits were compared to mine. I felt compelled to be mindful of creating the least emotional baggage possible for them. I was rather detached in those days, though I was tuned in to other people enough to know that many things, which did not affect me emotionally, affected others. I certainly did not want to be the one to scar my soft-hearted and sensitive children by inadvertently misunderstanding them.

My children formed a reasonable chunk of my initial research into personality traits. As they grew older, their individuality became more apparent and unbelievably accurate to their depictions in astrology. I became passionate about this insight and wished everyone knew how much easier it is to have smooth interactions with loved ones when we understand the inherent differences in the people around us, especially those in our close realms.

I observed myself after that reading. The drive to know more increased and I needed to understand how I ticked. I was fascinated - it was as though a whole new world of possibility was presenting itself to me. Sure enough, synchronicity took care of the steps. Within a week of my reading, I was grocery shopping and walked past a large table of books on display outside a newsagent. A small paperback book about astrology caught my eye. I picked it up and flicked through the pages searching for my star sign of Aquarius.

The format of this book was like no other that I had ever seen; it had deliberately listed the traits associated with each star sign, starting with the positive and followed by the less desirable ones. I read the list for Aquarius and was astounded; it was as if for the first time I recognised myself. I was stunned then (and now, as I write this sentence, I am teary) to see how each listed trait resonated with me so strongly. I had never before associated myself with these descriptive words, and they invoked feelings mostly of pride, modesty, and others – including embarrassment. As I read the descriptions I was enveloped in a deep all-consuming comfort, and I felt satisfied with who I was. I had forgotten many of the exceptional things I was capable of. Each of the distinguishing qualities on that list assured me that there was nothing wrong with me and that certain attributes which I viewed as negative were in fact wonderful. Some characteristics assured tremendous natural skills and idiosyncrasies, all of which I resonated with. I considered every trait and dissected its meaning in detail, recalling scenarios in my life where they had played out. I easily acknowledged almost every single adjective listed, based on myself. I even had to own the negative ones - some made me gasp, to realise that I was capable of them. I was. That admission was confronting. Still, I could not deny the truth. This was me and I was alright. I liked me!

Given that book was generalised and based on each star sign, I was sensible enough to know that I was not the only Aquarian person in the world and that fact intrigued me. I wondered how all people born under this star sign could possibly be similar to me, or as the list indicated, potentially the same.

My interest in the psyche of people escalated as I embarked on a researching frenzy. I had to know for myself. Could these traits, which were so accurate for me, possibly fit for all people born under the same sign?

First, I probed those closest to me - my husband, Mum, Dad and my kids. I did not stop there; once I scrutinized my family members, I continued delving into the persona of my friends. When I finished with them I turned my investigation to acquaintances and then strangers. I was eager to gather as much affirmation as possible. Whenever I was in any social situation, seated next to a stranger on public transport, in class or in my workplace, I asked what their star sign was. Most knew, the usual response after they told me was, "What does that mean?" or "Is it good?" I always responded with, "They are all good!"

Following on from my study of the essential nature of people, my inquiry turned to the interaction between the various star signs. Certain star signs are more complementary to the natural identity while other signs are challenged by differences. Some combinations interact peacefully, and other ones will trigger a more provoking interaction, simply based on the innate behaviour each sign exudes.

When I approached people with star signs not ideally aligned with mine, I was faced with their dismay at my questions. Some believed that astrology was not reliable, or just plain bullshit. I quickly ascertained the star signs most likely to react in this manner.

Most people were happy to participate in my survey, answering questions while I gathered data, filing it all in my mind. I studied by observation, and followed up with questions to affirm or deny my findings. I was never shy to approach a complete stranger, if I had been observing them, to ask their sign and discover if their behaviour or physical appearance fit with my assimilation. Sometimes I was wrong, but most times my perception was correct. I also read astrology books; however, I found it so much easier to interact experientially to witness if character traits and behavioural patterns fit.

During my obsessive astrology-analysis phase, my sister-in-law gifted me with a set of tarot cards. I had a vague idea what they were as I put them on my bookshelf, where they remained untouched for five years. I was preoccupied with my young family and work, leaving little time to delve. Later, they were my introduction to energy, to the intuitive power we hold within. They highlighted the intelligence of our soul.

Every year my friend and I looked forward to our annual psychic reading with Jason MacDonald. He was so renowned we had to wait twelve months for our turn! It was always worth the wait, and I was given information that did not make sense until many years later. Some observations were irrelevant at the time, but later when they played out in my life, I would be reminded by a thought of when I had been told previously. As the years passed, much of the information he shared with me eventuated, making me more certain that our lives are planned. Occasionally I saw a different reader in-between the annual reading, all of whom consistently assured me that I was clairvoyant or psychic or "like them." For about ten years I made no assimilation with this statement. I simply did not recognise these skills in myself.

Turns out my understanding of what being psychic meant was different to the reality. I had the impression that a psychic could see, as if watching a film, events that would come true. My misguided impression of intuitive energy had manifested through movies, along with the negative representation and clichés often associated with these types. They were often portrayed as manipulators, con artists, and charlatans wearing flowing gowns while gazing into a crystal ball, telling people when they would die.

My actual knowledge of clairvoyance and psychic phenomenon went only as far as the readers I sought guidance from, and for the most part I was impressed with what they knew about me, my life and family. My experiences were positive. They did not mention death, and I did not misconstrue information they passed on to me or wait for things to happen. I found solace in their guidance, and most of it was affirmation of what I already sensed. If I received a reading which did not resonate with me then I simply forgot about it.

During this phase, I was aware that my mother saw "people" around her bed at night sometimes, which fascinated me. However, she never made a big deal out of it, and only casually mentioned whenever it occurred every once in a while.

I later discovered that I was able to do this "psychic stuff" very well; in fact, intuition and deciphering energy morphed into the foundations of my purpose.

In the early 2000's, whilst reconnecting with myself, I experienced a time of intense personal growth. I continued regaining my identity by meeting my most dominant challenge of practicing assertiveness by sharing my feelings. With any change came side effects, especially when resetting boundaries. Once I began to state my preferences honestly, my husband became confused, as in the past I always went along with whatever he suggested. These adjustments came left of field for him, especially given he was unaware that anything was wrong in the first place. I had never indicated there was.

My husband relied on me to take care of anything to do with the household, family, my work, and his business - though he only expected that because I had never asked him to help me. He had no indication that I needed assistance as I carried out all family tasks with precision and ease. I did not know it was acceptable to ask him to help me. I justified that he worked hard, while never acknowledging that I did too. In my attempt to regain a more even distribution of tasks, I asked him to make phone calls for his business himself instead of calling me to make them. These small gestures made sense. They required minimal adjustment by both of us and I was determined to relieve myself of some of the everyday chores and expectations that I had created.

My soul-searching phase meant I recalled many things that were said to me over the years. It was not so much the exact words that mattered, but these off-handed comments shut me down. Certain statements facilitated me evolving into a passive personality who chose to shut up rather than risk feeling rejected, to cover up my sensitivity and fear of being disliked. Without realising it I slowly stopped being my true self.

One of those recollections was not long after Rade and I started to date when I was 21. We were in the car chatting together, and I was sharing how I believed a situation for one of our friends would turn out. He became annoyed, telling me to stop predicting. Perhaps I came across as a know it all? I never protested or defended my observations or expressed my strong sense on the matter. What I did was stop sharing with him. I felt humiliated, being scolded like a child, and I had no intention of allowing it to happen again. My guard was up, and I was careful with what I said when sharing my feelings and senses. I realise now that I had strong intuitive ability; however, to avoid judgement, I quietened my observations, effectively putting the real me to sleep.

All I had to do was state my cause by saying I believed what I felt to be true about our friend, but I did not have the courage to do that, and instead, fell into victim mode. I was sure I had been shut down, made to feel inferior and stupid. The reality is, no one can make us feel any way; we react because of our own insecurities. You see, I already believed I was stupid due to my lack of further education. If we do not believe about ourselves what others insinuate, their comments will have little or no effect on us.

One thing for sure: life with my husband was a contrast to my freedom-filled childhood days with my family. This had a major effect on me since, as a child, I felt accepted - at least by my immediate family, the ones that I looked up to. I had taken his remark to heart, and for sharing my thoughts I now felt isolated, embarrassed and insecure, believing that what I thought did not matter. This one comment put a large dent in my self-worth and fostered my pattern to stop speaking out. Now I was mindful of what I shared with my husband about my insights, opinions or what I believed in.

Thankfully I was able to speak openly with my two lifelong friends. Conversation is extremely important to me, and at the early stage in our marriage relationship, I was already starting to deny my voice.

I felt stupid, not smart. Not clever at all. And remarks from my husband or kids referencing how I finished school in junior levels highlighted my own dire recognition of my lack of education. I believed that my husband had created this summary of me, and in my mind I heard his comments as, *"You are dumb."* The truth is he never once said anything of the sort. His references to my schooling were true and they triggered a deep-seated fear in me that I was not good enough. I already believed that about myself before partnering with him.

During this phase of regaining some sense of self I underwent Myers-Briggs psychological testing. My friend worked in recruitment and had access to comprehensive tests to assist her company to recruit high-end employees. When I sat for the tests, they were for personality, looking at how I interacted with people, as well as IQ testing to gauge general intelligence, ability to perceive knowledge and process information. My results were great. That testing killed any insecurity I had around my intellect. When I proudly announced my results, my husband said he knew I was intelligent. That stupid insecurity was mine alone, it was not caused by him. How liberating to discover that I was clever and not stupid! I felt euphoric and my confidence soared.

My obsession with getting to know myself while studying other people continued. Not many people came to our home to visit, as my husband was quite withdrawn. Although I was used to the way that he was, for visitors it may have appeared rude and unwelcoming. I grew up in an interactive family enjoying each other's company, whereas my husband preferred to hide out on his own, avoiding social situations. His withdrawal and introversion manifested as deep loneliness for me.

In an attempt to cover up my loneliness and unconscious lack of control over where my life was at, I cleaned. I kept our home pristine, not so much clean as tidy. When my children were small I swooped to collect their toys, putting them away the moment they had finished. I had everything in our house in order; at least on the surface, my home looked very organised to the extent that I could maintain it. I lived with a hoarder; I was a minimalist, while if there was a clear space, my husband put something on it.

I discovered that we cover up parts of our psyche which we are inadvertently avoiding. We do this by distraction, using excessive behaviour as the tool. Mine was tidying; for others, they might be a gym junkie, social butterfly, clean freak, shopaholic or anything that plays out beyond moderation. One way or another, when we do anything to excess we are compensating for an area of our life where we feel like we have no control or have lost it.

In February 2006, I travelled overseas on the spur of the moment. A good friend of mine dropped in to visit and mentioned he was travelling to Egypt. Ever since I was young I felt drawn to Egypt. In a few short weeks my passport, flights, and trip were organised and I set off on my first international adventure on my own. I was thirty-five years old. I landed in Cairo to discover there were guards with machine guns slung over their shoulder at the airport, a contrast to my country; however, I did not find it intimidating. I felt surprisingly comfortable. I found a driver to take me to my hotel in the middle of the city and spent the first night in Egypt alone, waiting for Graeme to arrive the next day. I was happy to see him, not because I was afraid, but I looked forward to company and experiencing this country with someone whom I could discuss the adventure with. This was the first non-Western country I had visited so everything was fascinating; the crazy driving with no regard to road rules (accompanied by incessant honking of horns) and so many people, predominantly men, everywhere.

Graeme met a man at the airport who offered to be our tour guide and drive us around to all the sights for a day. Our guide took us to his associates, who took tourists across the desert to the pyramids on camelback. For a negotiated price we set off to explore the Pyramids of Giza, riding a camel with a young man guiding us across the vast sandy desert where the wind blasted us with sand. It was hard to keep my eyes open. The Great Pyramids were spectacular - an incredible display which left me in awe, wondering how they were constructed. My observation of energy around them was blurred; the powerful spiritual history seemed mild. Survival among the local people meant tourism provided a necessary outlet that, in my opinion, has taken its toll on the energetic sacredness.

There are guards whom you can pay a dollar, granting permission to do whatever you wish inside and around the pyramids. While photography is not allowed, paying a small bribe entitles you to take photos inside the pyramids or even take pieces of them. I was in the early stages of waking up to energy and felt it was not right to take photos inside. However, outside I had my picture taken with a guard, featuring his machine gun, in front of one of the giant stones of the Pyramid of Giza.

Exploring the ancient land raised a different kind of awareness in me. I realised how materialistic Westerners can be in comparison to these people. My impression was that they adequately survive with limited ingredients or possessions. Life appeared simplistic and the people seemed content, proud of their country and heritage. The overall energy, even in the heart of this huge bustling city, was calm, emanating from the men as each individual went about their day in peace.

When I returned home to Australia, a major shift had taken place within me. I became conscious of the enormity of possessions we have: clothing, vehicles, toys, the size of our homes, all of this beamed at me for the first time. I was ashamed. I stopped shopping for things that were not necessary and I lost any desire to keep up with other people. I stopped watching television, for suddenly the programs came across as contrived. It took little effort to disconnect from spending time engrossed in the manipulative propaganda orchestrated in the media as I started noticing what was really important.

Following my life-changing light bulb moment, which inspired personal transformation, I pondered the synchronicity of meeting Graeme. When I was nineteen I shared a house with friends. One moved out, and the guy who owned the house advertised for a new housemate. Graeme was a thirty-year-old enigma who moved in with a cardboard box that stored his few possessions. He was physically active, loathed being tied to regular work, and had aspirations to do something more meaningful than his fitter and turner trade. He was studying to work with people. Years later when we reconnected, he worked with wayward teens, and he was brilliant at it. Being a free spirit, I never knew when I might hear from him. He occasionally turned up at my home, always random, just as he had done when he mentioned he was off to Egypt when I hijacked his trip. He has to be a significant soul alliance for me.

I will know for sure once I leave this body if he is part of my soul family. Our soul reincarnates with other souls, and during meditation we can recognise them. You may recall when meeting someone for the first time, feeling comfortable, as though you have known each other for ages. This is a strong indication that your souls have been together in other lifetimes.

My husband and I had been actively participating in a Groundhog Day scenario every week since almost the beginning of our time together, which now amounted to sixteen years. We discussed our silent treatment pattern and the consequent withdrawal that took place in our home every week, even discussing the lack of resolution. The fact that we were talking meant that we were speaking again and the silence was broken. The unfortunate reality is that neither of us were aware that the underlying issues were much deeper and that nothing changes until something new is implemented.

The way for us was a vicious cycle, which seemed like this to me: I would say something either mundane, or important, or simply be too laid back with the kids. There was no particular outstanding trigger, but the usual response was my husband retreating to our bedroom and we would not speak for a couple of days.

I played a part in the silence as well, each time this happened, always wondering what I had done. My mind raced with thoughts that I had not done anything. I never understood why I was in trouble. I felt sorry for myself as I sat there obsessing over the latest situation, pondering what I did. Logically, I knew I had not done anything; but I was not emotionally mature enough to ascertain that not everything was about me. I was super-sensitive and took every single retreat personally. So circumstances that were not caused by me, in my mind *were* caused by me; and because my husband never shared his feelings about why he withdrew, I never knew that I was not the cause.

My pattern during a period of the silent treatment always shifted from sadness and overthinking in an attempt to understand what exactly I had done to cause it. Then I would transition into anger as I reassured myself that I was nice, low-maintenance, undemanding, loving, kind, and did not deserve this silence. My inability to communicate any of this to my husband meant I became more and more bitter, assuming that he was angry at me. The situation was never about me; however, I was angry at myself and my inability to discuss my fears or share my feelings. What a silly never-ending cycle!

There I was, feeling like a lonely victim. Most nights of the week I spent sitting on the couch wondering what was wrong with me. My thoughts were that something must be seriously wrong with me, as my husband did not want to sit with me or have a conversation. Rade left for work early in the morning and returned in time to eat dinner. Usually, without waiting for the kids and I to finish eating, he would leave the table and retreat to the bedroom, either to go to sleep or to be on the computer. The loneliness I felt over all those years was intense.

There were times that my husband went away for a weekend or a night to enjoy his hobbies of collecting old things or looking at vintage cars. Each time, either one or both of my two best friends came to stay with me to make the most of an opportunity to catch up. Those times together with my friends lifted my spirits immensely. I have always been able to be myself with them. We talked, we danced, we laughed, and always had fun together, making everything else more bearable.

It was many years after our marriage relationship dissolved that I discovered the silent treatment we were engulfed in was never actually about anything I had said. It was, at the core, a passive-aggressive representation of low self-worth. Over sixteen years nothing changed as we continued to play out the same pattern, never resolving our behaviour or delving to discover why we did it. It was the ultimate demise of our relationship, breaking our marriage, long before it ended.

LIFE LESSON #6
We are energetically equal.

To realise that you are energetic is comforting and empowering, though being in touch with the energetic aspects of yourself is not where your power lies. In life, wisdom arrives through deciphering your own human spirit, which is the essence of self-awareness. Contentment that comes from liking yourself is the most generous gift of life; with it, you are freed from stressing about what others think of you and you can feel comfortable with your appearance and personality.

Life Actions

1. Do you consider your culture better off than another culture?

2. Do you become angry or sad when injustice or disaster strikes?

3. Do you believe that homeless people are less or more evolved as souls?

**Connect with Toni and get
free resources to support you!**

www.ToniReillyInstitute.com/awake-bonus

CHAPTER 7:
MAJOR LIFE CHANGES

Although it was a slow process, there was an intangible force driving me to change my patterns, to seriously address the way I communicated with my husband. My first outburst (complete with tears) erupted when my third child, Coco, was 18 months old. I worked full-time doing accounts for a small company in Brisbane. Bebe was five and in pre-school. Reo was four, and Coco was two; both were in child care. Weekdays started between 4 or 5 a.m. when Coco woke up, when I leaped out of bed preparing breakfast for the kids, dressing them, brushing teeth, fixing hair, packing their bags, then showering in preparation for a full day of work. After buckling the kids into their respective seats I dropped them at two separate child care centres each morning - except for Tuesday, when I had to drop all three at different venues and be at work by 8 a.m.!

This crazy daily run-around left no time to enjoy quality time interacting with my kids. If they were sad or distressed or wanted to show me something they made at school, mostly it was barely recognised because I had to run. When Coco was at that fill-in day care centre she always looked lost; it was heart-wrenching leaving her there, but I had no time to stop and dwell or to become emotionally entrenched. I had to keep going, literally. That was hard.

My husband was separate from all of this. He was not involved in the daily routine. Not once did he drop or collect our children from childcare. I never asked him to. Noticing other fathers were involved in the daily scrabble made me realise that it was possible to have balance, and that helping each other was normal in other people's relationships. I followed my mother's example to my own detriment: in our home, taking care of the housework, our children, and my husband. In my lunch break I went to the supermarket to buy groceries so that after work I could go straight to collect my tired children and go home for the evening routine. It was a never-ending roundabout of action. I was on autopilot.

One evening I burst into tears, telling my husband that I was overwhelmed with all that I had to do. The combination of household chores, with all the running around for our children, and full-time employment, was too much. We had been together for almost 10 years and this was the first time that I recall losing it. I admitted to myself that I had a heavy schedule to carry. When I expressed my distress to Rade, he hugged me and told me he was proud of me and of all that I did for him and our family. He was not aware of what a day in my life consisted of since I did not share the details. He wanted to know what he could do to help me. On the rare occasion that I did gather the courage to raise with him anything that bothered me, he was always understanding and offered to help. He believed if his wife was happy the whole family is happier. So he did his best to accommodate that outcome.

By the time I had gathered enough courage to show my distress, I was wound up by years of pent-up internalised anger. It astounded me that it was not obvious to my husband all that I did in the home. Instead of relief I felt even worse; now I had created another job for myself. I had to instruct my husband on what to do and when. I fumed internally, running over in my mind that I already was responsible for planning and managing our three children, myself, my husband, his business, my work and now I had to add in another job so that he could assist me. I dutifully looked after everyone and saw allocating chores at that stage as another chore. I obsessed on why he could not see what needed to happen to run this family. So I continued doing everything myself, justifying that by the time I instructed Rade, it was less hassle to simply do things myself.

I was my own worst enemy. My husband could not win, as I became more tightly entwined in my suffering, continually adding to the buildup of internalised bitterness. I believed it was my husband who caused my anger, and still my aggravation remained unexpressed, gathering even more momentum as frustration. Eventually it dawned on me that it was myself who I was angry at, disappointed at my inability to express and voice my feelings and fears. This was my challenge, not his. To a certain extent he was an innocent bystander, copping the energetic brunt of my unexpressed fury.

In my mind it was blatantly obvious that I needed help, and even more clear what needed to be done. I rarely sat down other than to eat dinners; there was no time to stop from 4 or 5 a.m. in the morning until 7 p.m. at night when I put our three kids to bed. I started to become bitter at my husband. I recognised anger and frustration building up in me from time to time, but kept it pent up inside.

I obsessed over why Rade did not contemplate the many things I carried out, believing that he could choose to help me, if he wanted to. Instead of asking him, I developed stories in my head, that he must be avoiding these noticeable tasks to annoy me deliberately. The truth is he was genuinely oblivious. He explained how he required instructions, that none of this was obvious to him, while assuring me that he would happily do anything I asked of him. I had not communicated what I needed, or asked for help; so how would he know?

My attitude changed a little from then, at least internally. Deep down I knew I was responsible for where I was in my life, but that did not stop me from feeling like a victim. I felt like I had no support in daily life. My parents lived more than a thousand kilometres away, my close girlfriends had their own busy lives, and all were unaware of my feelings, as I did not say anything to them. Whenever we caught up, the last thing I wanted to talk about was kids and family. More than anything I relished a break, precious time with them to be an adult and feel worthwhile, free to be myself without responsibility or anyone to take care of for a few hours.

My mother was quietly observing my personal demise, though she held back from sharing her observations with me. She was on the outside looking in. My oppression was obvious; however, I only discovered what she witnessed after my separation, as both my parents shared their relief with me. You see, in their eyes, I could do no wrong; so my parent's perspective is one-sided. They were on my side. They always have been.

From the time I gave birth to our three children I do not recall once sitting together with my husband on our couch. In the evening when the kids went to bed, I was relieved to revert to being an adult, spending the evenings watching television on my own. It was the same routine every night. I was desperately lonely. I craved companionship. I wished that my husband would sit with me, enjoy a glass of wine, engage in conversation and debrief about our day. To add to feeling taken for granted, I wanted to be noticed, to receive attention. I wished my partner was my friend.

A big part of my loneliness was self-inflicted, a side-effect of my struggle to speak up, which in turn stemmed from my dread of instigating the silent treatment. There were as many nights spent on the couch on my own feeling lonely, as ones where I cried to myself wondering what I had done this time to deserve silence from Rade. About half of any given week and most weekends were spent in silence. It was torture.

I was well and truly trapped in a deep abyss of sad, deep loneliness which was relentless (at least when I was at home). I did not know how to get out; it certainly never occurred to me that I could leave my marriage. The idea of counselling never entered my sphere as an option either. It took several years of feeling oppressed, enduring the silent treatment, slipping into an angry space inside, feeling victimised, and thinking that I did not deserve this treatment. I justified that I was a good person. I never made waves, carried out all the domestic tasks, and never challenged or disagreed with Rade. Still, he retreated in silence. I simply did not understand, ensuring there was no solution in sight. I did not discuss this with anyone, so I remained deeply ingrained in my funk.

About two years before our marriage ended, in yet another discussion about the silent treatment and with me crying in frustration, Rade listened, seemed to understand and even made changes; still, every week it would end up silent in our house. The changes were surface solutions, not achievable for a long-term cure, as neither of us possessed awareness of what fuelled our behaviour at the core. We both knew that something drastic had to happen. At some point we said out loud that separation was becoming inevitable. I don't think either of us ever believed separation would actually eventuate.

I craved romance and attention. I was desperate to feel appreciated. I wanted to be noticed, and most of all, I wanted to be seen and heard. I was looking for acknowledgement. Mostly I did not know how to express what I was feeling, so being heard by him was only ever available on a superficial level. My wishes were hidden, though very alive in my mind. I rarely revealed the deep emotions that encompassed me. I feared judgement. My worst fear was to be viewed as high-maintenance, which created internal struggle and continued to degrade my self-worth. All by myself on that couch was the only place the build-up of anger inside could be released, in the form of silent tears and incessant recurring thoughts. I felt sorry for myself.

In a quest to improve our marriage, around the time Rade turned 40, our kids were old enough to stay with his mother and we started to go out a little bit. All of his school friends were turning 40 that year, which meant there were lots of party invitations. We enjoyed ourselves, breaking the cycle of always being at home in a routine. We also placed more emphasis on re-igniting our sex life. I wanted intimacy to be a part of our lives again and for us to pay attention to our physical needs. For years, all three children turned up in the middle of the night to hop into our bed, with all five of us squashed together. There was no chance of lovemaking, so I trained the kids to stay in their own beds to allow intimacy back into our relationship.

Together we managed to revamp things between us, bringing the spark back into our relationship. Our sex life was active again; it was fun, even more fulfilling than it used to be. It was better because I was more comfortable than ever with spicy physical fun. Our relationship grew stronger, we were more romantic than we had ever been. But it was not enough to keep us together forever.

Through my study of human nature, including innate characteristics, I learned that Rade was never going to be overly social, making my only option to accept him. It was not a deal-breaker; however, socialising and interacting with people was who I was, through and through. I became compelled to make changes to my lifestyle and took responsibility for making adjustments. For the first time I put energy into seeking out social gatherings, starting with events other parents from school were involved in.

While out, I observed other couples and they appeared equal. I noticed when a husband asked his wife about her day, and I noted how social certain couples were. I craved a relationship like these. I did not make the association until much later but what I was doing was envying what I perceived these couples had together and comparing it with what I did not have with Rade. I felt like I was missing out. The truth is, these relationships had their troubles, too; but I was blinded to their problems, choosing to only see what was missing from mine.

Meanwhile, Rade was doing his best to please me, even coming out with me sometimes. Usually he left early, so I used to stay on my own. This became the new standard for us and I did not mind. I was deliriously happy to be out, behaving like an adult again, socialising, laughing and conversing. I had missed out on these things for many years.

Alarm bells began ringing when I was introduced to a woman at a school function. She was there without a partner so I asked where her husband was. She told me she no longer had one and I responded with, "Oh you are so lucky!" Later that night I realised my brazen comment might have been out of line. I hoped that she was not widowed! I checked with my new friend to see what happened, fearing I may have put my foot in my mouth with my outburst. I discovered that she and her husband were separated. She had three children who were similar ages to mine and we became great friends. Little did I know that I would soon be in the same situation.

Had I been able to express myself, things could potentially have been very different between us. Rade was a great listener; he was a deeply feeling, softhearted man who unfortunately (like me) was unable to express his emotions. Rade's parents fought and argued throughout his childhood, so he decided he was not going follow their lead in his own marriage. He took it to the extreme by never raising his voice, ever; instead, he resorted to passive-aggressive responses. I interpreted his silent withdrawal as, "It is not acceptable to disagree with him" – otherwise, he would retreat. The dreaded silent treatment became constant in our relationship.

Our life together was nice in many ways, the times when we

were not in a silence, we were like friends; affectionate, loving and respectful of each other. The outward appearance of our relationship portrayed a perfect couple - a very different story to the lonely oppression I chose to keep hidden deep inside my heart.

All I wanted was to be free of my routine, free from the boundaries of fitting in with my husband. My kids were easygoing. I took great care of them and they always went with the flow. I became aware more than ever of my need to be more assertive, to say what I wanted, to share what I liked to do. Being authentic and honest enough to speak from my heart was a huge challenge for me. I was consumed by worry, wondering what Rade would think of me. My biggest fear of all was appearing needy. Such a paradox! I was desperately in need, yet emotionally crippled with fear of being vulnerable.

Rade went away for three weeks working interstate, allowing me to experience being on my own with my children. Those weeks were a blessing. I was under no pressure to behave in any particular way or to prepare meals at a certain time. I relaxed, relieved from the obligation to consider my husband's needs. I was free of responsibility to be at home on a tight schedule. I spent some of those afternoons with my new friends. All of our children went to the same school, so they were more than happy hanging out together, and so were we.

A critical turning point arrived, bringing clarity: that I must take responsibility for my hopes and dreams. I weighed up our relationship, pondering the state of my life, reflecting the notion of how I would feel if things were still the same in five years' time. I was not willing to find out.

An internal force compelled me to alter the incessant recurring patterns I had become so accustomed too. I sat down to write a long letter to my husband, explaining in detail how I felt. I wrote about my deep sadness, loneliness and feeling taken for granted. I admitted that I had no idea how to avoid the silent withdrawal. I acknowledged his heartwarming attempts to please me, explaining that he would only be capable of upholding certain changes for a short period, as his new behaviours, as much as I appreciated them, were outside of his innate character. In that very long letter I kept all references about me. I knew enough to resist placing blame on him, but to focus on the way that I felt. I reached clarity in my psyche, steadfast in the knowledge that I had created my own oppression, not him.

As I write this paragraph my chest constricts and tears stream down my face, recalling how painful it was to give my husband - the man that I loved - that letter, knowing that our lives would never be the same again. His initial reaction was calm, although hurt. He assured me of his willingness to do whatever it took to improve our relationship so that we could stay together. He agreed to move out to allow me some space to think. The time had come to decide what I wanted. As painful as that guilt-saturated period was, my relief was impossible to deny. The liberation was overwhelming, making me certain that we would not reunite.

When we separated our friends and family were shocked. They were under the impression that we had a strong marriage, believing we were the perfect couple. We appeared that way, but it goes to show how different the reality lives can be, compared to what is portrayed. People assume, never knowing what it is like to be in the relationship. Only the two people in it know the truth.

Leaving my husband was an intense, emotionally traumatic time in my life, the first of this calibre. The decision created a catalyst for a complete swing in the direction my life went in. I was overwhelmed by guilt, for hurting my husband and kids. I wondered how they would cope. Guilt haunted me for years. Logically I understood that I was not responsible for how he felt or how he came to be who he is, but this knowledge did not override my empathy; it only ensured the intensity of the guilt that I harboured. Polarities took hold when on one hand I was ecstatic, liberated, finally free to be myself, relieved to release the burden of living a raging lie; while on the other hand, I was fraught with sadness and extreme sorrow for my husband. Living with the knowledge that his devastation was caused by my decision to end our marriage was tough. I sobbed at night, swirling in a deep pool of culpability, never revealing my distress to anyone.

Externally I showed a smiling face, keeping my emotional turmoil hidden. Who would be interested in that? I never allowed anyone to see my deep feelings of self-condemnation, not even when people occasionally voiced their assumptions on how great life must be for me, given that I chose to split-up. My reclaimed freedom was fraught with paradoxical waves of elation and emotional havoc.

It was some time after our marriage ended that my search for self-awareness led me to understand that low self-esteem was the main cause of the silent retractions which featured in our relationship. I was acutely aware that it is not possible to change a person at their core; an introvert will not become an extrovert. Certain characteristic traits are innate, and they form the basis of who we are. Other characteristic traits are learned. I concluded that some of Rades' ways were innate, no longer fitting well with mine. Like me, Rade had bruises from childhood, which were triggered, steering the learned behaviours that played out between us.

Going our separate ways produced a shift in awareness, with the fallout creating major wake up calls for both of us. One of the saddest revelations was how I was rarely present with my kids. I was so damned busy with the practical aspects of life that I did not register how distracted I was with my own feelings. I was too consumed with myself to be in the moment with them. Changes were underway as circumstances created this opportunity to rediscover myself, to reclaim my identity and to be more attentive with my kids.

Life would never be the same again for my husband, our

children or me.

Guilt entered my psyche heavily from this point and haunted me deeply with its all-encompassing wrath. It is more than ten years since this point and that is how long it has taken me to work through my guilt.

Our life is destined.

Our lives are a blueprint. My marriage ended as per my life map. No judgment or trying harder would have worked because those are human actions inspired by morals or "the right thing to do" - they have no real power over the destined plan. Of course, they do challenge us, precisely as they are meant to. At the point anything ends, the learning phase ramps up.

Life Actions

1. If you are in a difficult relationship, have you taken the time to withdraw, to be alone, to get enough distance to gain clarity for making your own choices?

2. Do you often ask for advice or base your moves on what others think or tell you to do, rather than finding your own way?

3. Whether you decide to stay or go, have you taken responsibility for following your own plan – not someone else's?

**Connect with Toni and get
free resources to support you!**

www.ToniReillyInstitute.com/awake-bonus

CHAPTER 8:
LOVE AT FIRST SIGHT

Love is the strongest energetic force of all. A fated union drives us to be with that special someone no matter who or what stands in the way. The desire to be with the person we love takes over all senses of logic, ensuring our priorities become blurred. When a special love arrives the connection is reciprocated with feelings so intense they border on euphoric, making anyone else invisible. When we meet this person love makes us blind to personal traits, obscuring insecurities along with the challenges the relationship united to overcome. Initially we see only the best in the other. Both parties restrain themselves, revealing their best qualities to impress the person they love. We compromise so our insecurities remain in the background until they can no longer be hidden. Timing of events and circumstances ensure our true self, flaws and all eventually surface.

I have experienced love on several levels. I am referring to love between lovers as opposed to the love we feel for family or friends. My first relationships as a teenager I categorise more as crushes, as my fascination with those boys wore off quickly. The man I married was my first love. When I left after 16 years, the relationship following became an amplified version. All my emotions with this connection were intensified; I did not know it was possible to feel so deeply for another person. Until people have a similar experience, they may judge what others do and how they manage their own commitments. Rest assured, when a fated love union arrives neither party will be able to resist or stop the process, as it takes on a powerful force of its own.

How many people believe that if they commit to marriage then they must stay in the relationship for life? Cultural dictation and religious doctrines teach with emphasis on sticking it out in a marriage. Our conditioned beliefs infringe on feelings; we rule with our logic, disregarding when the in love feeling wanes, ignoring our lack of fulfilment as we continue the relationship, believing there is no other option while we live under the guise of morals as an obligation to "do the right thing."

The way I see it, before we arrive our life is planned; there is a map in place which we often only ever know subconsciously. The script for each of our lives includes all the people and circumstances that we experience, with markers presented in the form of triggers, to ensure that our destined scenes are acted out. They play out without us realising there is a plan.

Life is a production: we are all cast to perform a role which we act out unwittingly until the aftermath is revealed. The reason behind an experience is only ever evident in hindsight. If we realised the purpose and knew exactly what to do or say there would be no need to be here on earth. Once it seems natural to search for deeper meaning in any situation, the answers become obvious - especially when we look at other people's lives. The challenge is harder when we try to recognise it in our own existence.

My perspectives on life are not presented to make excuses for non-virtuous behavior. Nor is it so that we can do whatever we desire with no regard for other people. I believe in taking responsibility for our actions and that all actions have consequences. Morals, on the other hand, exist only because they are placed on us by enforcing staged rules for what is right and wrong as influenced by society, church, school, and passed on by our parents.

We come together to discover specific insights from each other, the lesson structured to achieve a specific result. The nature of our relationship, the unique traits of both people, combined with our individual lives and background prior to meeting, will bring to the surface the best and worst in one another.

The face we show, the personality we allow friends, family, peers and colleagues to see is carefully upheld; but a partner is witness to another side of us, one that is only shown to them. A partner inadvertently or intentionally triggers certain responses. They usually do not understand that our reactions stem from buried fears of insecurity, feelings of abandonment, betrayal, humiliation, rejection or unfairness. The very nature of living with someone and being intimate nurtures a whole other dynamic, which we will never have with anyone who is not a lover.

My work with people allowed me the means to observe human behaviour in a way that is pure. My clients felt no need to hide anything from me and willingly shared their secret stories, which some may see as immoral. No one is bad; we are people colliding with fated unions, prescribed to incorporate experiences to challenge the core of our being, forcing us into discomfort in order to overcome and learn.

What kind of things are we learning? The main purpose of the human experience is to navigate emotions. Emotion does not exist when we are not in a body. In our energetic form our thoughts, knowledge, insight, and traits are highlighted for every other soul to see. Our energy is transparent; we cannot hide anything, nor is there any need to. Our soul has nothing to defend, nothing to compete for or to envy; there is only peace and acceptance. We already know unconditional, non-judgemental tolerance, for this is the energy of where we are really from. Our soul energy is already pure. There is no shadow on the other side. Negativity is a human concept as is hierarchy. No person is better or worse than another because at the core we are all the same pure energetic force, simply here with a different agenda.

This chapter is about love at first sight: my pull towards destiny to meet an integral scene in my life, which challenged me to come closer to my mission.

Love is the strongest emotion that we are capable of feeling and it sets the scene for many other emotional experiences. Consider the breakdown of a relationship, where there are children involved, where one partner is still in love with their partner, while the other is no longer in love. The circumstances of the relationship ensure the one who is no longer in love experiences immense guilt. The scenario teaches about independence, freedom, strength and courage. The feelings I experienced may not be the same for everyone who has been through a similar separation, however this chapter is based on my responses.

My love story defied morals, with my real life encounter causing me to question every part of my psyche along with the human existence. On a humanitarian scale I came to understand that all people are driven by circumstances which are presented to them in order to live their purpose.

When I was in the sixteenth year together with my husband whom I loved, my best friend (Ness) and I decided to go on a "girls only" getaway interstate for a weekend. No partners or kids, just us. It was our chance to have some fun, to be free of responsibility for anyone except for ourselves for a couple of days. Long gone were the days where we went out or caught up at homes for meals, socialising, conversation, dancing and other fun occasions. Everything changed as life demanded our time with work and family. This trip was important to us. We went to great lengths arranging a three day leave pass from work and home. With our family commitments taken care of, and with flights and accommodation booked, we were all set for a fabulous weekend.

We flew out at lunch time on Friday for three whole nights and days all to ourselves, free of obligations or expectations. We planned to make the most of this time.

I was beside myself with excitement embracing the joy of feeling carefree the way I used to before I was married with children, prior to resuming responsibility for my family twenty-four hours a day, seven days a week.

Going away was my idea, as I had visited Melbourne eight years earlier to attend a wedding on my husband's side of the family. I perceived the city as cultured - the streets full of cafes, bars and restaurants, and there were eclectic people from all walks of life. St. Kilda was vibrant, filled with amazing places to eat, and my sister-in-law was the best host imaginable, showing me around. Melbourne had incredible energy; I felt as though I belonged there. Everything about it was in complete contrast to my mainstream life at home. The weather for starters - I was used to warm temperate weather year round, and this place had seasons. It was cold, literally freezing both outside and inside the flat where we stayed. Everything about that city appealed to me.

So, on this Friday eight years later, instead of our usual routine of dropping kids to daycare, school, working and preparing meals, my friend and I were on board a flight to Melbourne. To celebrate we ordered wine to emphasise our burst of freedom, enjoying every moment while we planned our weekend. On arrival at our hotel in the city we dropped our luggage and got dressed up, all set for an evening out.

After a fun and very social weekend with not a care in the world, we flew back to Brisbane to face our real lives. I remember telling her I did not want to go back to my real life! On landing my life resumed to the normal daily rush. My magical weekend away blurred quickly into the past. We made a pact to include a weekend to Melbourne as an annual treat to ourselves.

The weekend made me aware of how much I had lost myself. I was compelled to find myself again.

My intensive soul-searching phase was already underway, and the weekend spurred me to rediscover who I was. I was not being myself at home, so I decided it was high time to reclaim my identity. My life had slowly changed to such an extent that it happened without realising; now I felt driven to reactivate myself.

True to our pact, one year later, my friend and I set off for our second annual long weekend away in Melbourne. This time we were confident locals, since the three days exploring the city the previous year. We found a great place for lunch in the city and the afternoon passed quickly with our chatter. Being Friday, the venue became busier with people winding down, enjoying an end of the working week drink. With the venue pumping by now, two girls asked to sit at the spare seats on our table, so we took the opportunity to ask the girls to recommend some good places that we could head out to later. One of them wrote a list of three bars, which she labelled with a subtitle. The third bar on the list was "The Long Room" and she labelled it "the pick-up bar." Synchronicity was well underway, incredibly pertinent, though I had no idea at the time.

We caught a cab to the first place on the list, a nightclub; but when we arrived, there was a very long line of young people waiting to get inside. We waited for a while, declaring we were too old to bother waiting, when the group of people in line behind us announced they were giving this place a miss and heading around to another bar, which happened to be the third venue on our list. So we walked with them as they knew the way. I had no idea that I was following my intuition, allowing providence to unfold.

On arrival at The Long Room, I went to the bar for drinks. While waiting to be served I felt this surge of energy slap between myself and the person standing next to me. I turned to my left to see an extremely tall man standing beside me! I struck up small talk, asking about his height (which I am certain he must have endured all his life). Fascinated, I had to enquire - as I had never met anyone this tall before. He told me he was six foot eight and a bit. I was keen to keep talking, but the drinks arrived and my friend grabbed me to check out the place. We looked all around and found nothing overly exciting going on at The Long Room, so I asked her if we could find the tall man again. She agreed.

He was not hard to spot, so we headed over to his group and introduced ourselves. The conversation flowed immediately; we soon discovered that they were out to celebrate "wetting the baby's head." The tall man had become a father for the first time three weeks prior. Meanwhile, his friend was navigating a marriage breakdown, and since he was heartbroken over this, his buddies thought a night out would cheer him up and relieve the trauma he was going through.

These men were fun, great conversationalists, and easy to be around. My friend and I danced, talked, laughed and socialised into the early hours with them. I had no thought of going further than being social - until the end of the night, when the tall man came back to my hotel room with me. It felt strange, an unfamiliar act, something I had not done before; however, I did not stop myself, and I did not want to. My logic justified that no one would ever know.

The next day, my friend and I took this rare opportunity to laze around. We stayed in the hotel room instead of rushing into the day as we would usually do out of necessity, always up from 5 a.m. preparing for the day. My home life was relentless and a break was rare. That morning there was an INXS special on television, one of our favourite bands; so we lay about most of the day, singing along, laughing and recalling our fun from the night before.

As much as I tried, I could not get the tall man out of my head. He made an impression on me, especially in the short time we spent alone together. He consumed my thoughts.

Later in the day I decided to contact him, since we were going out for dinner, and I hoped he might join us. It took ages to compile a carefully written text, so when I went to attach his number to send the message I was devastated to find it was not stored in my phone. Given we were only in town for the weekend and these boys were local, he had given me his number, which I entered into my phone the night before while we were out. Perhaps too many to drinks was to blame for me not saving the number properly? I was disappointed but figured it must be meant to be, as I was well aware that contacting him was not the right thing to do.

My disappointment turned to excitement when I discovered the tall man's friend had given a business card to my friend. I asked her to call him to get his number for me. She was embarrassed and refused to make contact; but I wanted the number for the tall man, so I rang his friend. He answered, seeming very wary, and when I asked for the tall man's number, he told me he did not know it. Of course, he would protect his friends' anonymity. I was unusually pushy, though I eventually conceded by asking him to pass my number on. I thought that would be the end of it.

Nessie and I headed out for dinner to a street renowned for its ethnic restaurants. We chose a warm Italian place and were eating our meal when I received a text. The tall man! He wanted to meet us, and we agreed to meet at a pub later in the evening. I was beside myself with excitement, figuring it was harmless to meet again as we had so much fun the evening before. I justified I would go back interstate after the weekend, and his life would resume, so I should simply enjoy his company. Night Two away from normal life turned out to be another fun night of conversation, dancing, laughing and socialising with anyone who would talk to us, including the tall man.

The next day over breakfast out, Nessie and I pondered what to do for the day in this fabulous city. We decided to relive our youth with a Sunday afternoon session of live music, drinking and eating out, something we enjoyed often when we were younger, prior to the responsibility of being a mother became the main priority. We headed for an outdoor place in St. Kilda, one that we had been to on Sunday afternoon the previous year. We knew that it had live music and we found ourselves a great position, perfect for people-watching. We settled in for the afternoon, chatting, laughing, soaking up the sunny weather and relishing our precious free time. Although I wondered how it would be possible to arrange, I sent the tall man another text message, hoping that he could join us again. Sure enough, much later he came out to meet me.

As the weekend came to an end, while driving to the airport to return home, I felt reluctant to return to my real life. It was such a mess. The time had come to face up, stop making excuses and sort my marriage out. I returned home knowing that I had to separate from my husband. Those thoughts were reinforced when he went away for three weeks to work. It was a relief to be with my kids, having no particular dinner time or pressure to follow a tight schedule. It felt great, no other person to consider or tippy toe around. I could be myself with my kids.

The extent of meeting the tall man in Melbourne was my secret; still, I managed to talk about him constantly, telling my friends about this tall man who used to play professional sport when he was younger. He had a high profile so I was able to get away with mentioning him without suspicion that I was secretly enamoured. In my heart and logical mind I never believed that I would see or hear from him again.

A few weeks after that weekend in Melbourne, I received an email from the tall man. It came as a complete surprise; I never expected to hear from him. The content was devastating: he poured his heart out, sharing the shocking news that his friend, the heartbroken one whom we had spent the first night out with, had been killed in a freak accident.

The sudden unexpected death of his friend at the early age of thirty-nine, while in the prime of his life, had bought to the surface the realisation that his own life could be over in a second, creating a compulsion to assess his relationship. Most importantly, for the first time he looked at whether he was truly happy and fulfilled.

As I read the email through streaming tears, I felt sad for the loss of his friend, this warm, kind man whom I had only known for one single evening. I knew him long enough to be aware of the emotional turmoil he was experiencing around his wife leaving, trying to adjust to sharing the care of his children. He was gone now. I cried for the children who had lost their father, for the unresolved relationship breakdown, for the woman left behind to live with potential guilt and for not being able to experience closure.

I shed tears for the heartfelt feelings this man I hardly knew was expressing to me. Weighing up his life, and not knowing what was happening, his emotions were creating great confusion for him. He expressed that he knew exactly where his life was at, and where it was going, as he had everything planned - until he met me.

Many emails went back and forth between us, and what transpired was another weekend in Melbourne. I went to meet him again. I knew it was not ideal, certainly not acceptable in moral terms. It was sneaky, but I could not stop myself, I did not want to. All I could think about was what it would be when I saw him again.

As fate would have it, I was able to go to Melbourne for work and we arranged to meet. Six weeks had passed, so I had only a vague recollection of what he looked like. Still, I could hardly wait to see him. My heart was alight; I was bouncing with excitement, barely able to keep my secret.

As I opened the door to greet him, he took my breath away. I said out loud that he was even better than I remembered. We fell immediately into easy conversation, and later, passionate lovemaking, the likes of which I had never experienced before. We talked openly about our lives – well, at least I did, as my troubled marriage had been the main thing on my mind for the last few years. He, on the other hand, had been flowing along in his relationship not questioning if anything was missing, completely unaware (like me) that a deeper connection existed. Until now.

I asked about deciding to have a child at this later stage of life - both he and his partner were in their 40's - given that love did not seem to be a prominent aspect to their relationship. Based on what he shared, their partnership was driven by co-dependence and emotional manipulation. Together they appeared a couple who wished to show the world a perfect life, both with high achieving careers, living in the right area, owning all the right things to align with their ideal demographic and peers. He told me they decided to have a baby as it was now or never, given the body clock of his partner, and being at a stage where having a child would not be an option for much longer. Their child was meant to be.

Talking with the tall man spelled out loud and clear that all the dreams I had fantasised about while sitting on the couch on my own for the last eight years were actually possible. I realised that feeling lonely did not have to continue; there was more to life, a different life to the one I was currently leading.

My dreams were simple, I wished for someone to sit together in the evenings and talk and socially interact with me. I wanted to go out for coffee with them or enjoy it together at home. I wished for a partner who liked going out for dinner with me, and spending time with family and friends. I wished for someone who liked having friends in our home. I wished for someone who I could enjoy a glass of wine with. More than anything I wished for a companion, who was my lover and friend. I dreamed of all these things; they were missing from my life, along with feeling invisible most of the time. I had accepted that they were only wishes and believed they were not to be a part of my life. I believed that because I had married my husband, this was my lot to live. These thoughts consumed my mind most nights while I sat on the couch alone. In the eight years we lived in that home, I do not recall my husband sitting on the couch with me, not once.

All my negative thinking, feeling sorry for myself and lack of expression of my deep feelings was turning around at a fast pace. I studied my hopes and dreams in depth, the appeal of someone sharing the same simple things. Demonstrating genuine interest in me and what I had to say made my heart expand. What an incredible feeling! Exciting and liberating, all in one. I felt seen.

After that second meeting with the tall man I returned home and separated from my husband. I was not completely honest when I did not mention another man. I refused to be judged, or risk that our issues be blamed on someone else. I truly felt that that the tall man was not going to be in my life, he had his own family, and I had no desire to have a partner at that time. More than anything I wanted my freedom.

I craved to be free from oppression, free from feeling lonely, free from feeling like I was responsible for another adult. I was relieved that now I would only have to take care of myself and my three children in the way that I wanted to. I no longer needed to worry about being the way someone else wanted me to be or trying to be something that I thought I should be.

The emotional turmoil that I felt from this breakup was in complete opposition, the polarities immense. On one level the liberation of being free from daily pressure, the relief and happiness I felt was a ten. Finally I could be myself, run my life and my children the way that I wanted to. I am easygoing; I was not concerned about having a lot of money or building empires, all the things that were important to my husband that I was no longer a part of. The polarity was intense, deep-seated guilt, which encompassed me. I sobbed uncontrollably when I was on my own in bed at night. I felt gutted for this kind, sweet man, the father of my children whom I had left. This man who loved me. I never shared this with anyone.

I found it difficult to live with the devastation that my husband was feeling because of the breakdown of our marriage and the loss of our family unit in the traditional sense. I struggled with guilt associated with thoughts that perhaps I was a terrible mother. I believed that my choice to leave would scar my children emotionally for the rest of their lives. Even through this excruciating sadness and guilt, I could not go back. I knew it was the end of an era. My life would never be the same again.

I feel certain that we do not have complete control over our lives, at least not as much as we tell ourselves that we do; and neither are we victims. Free will is the culprit, the main factor of being human, ensuring that we behave as one. No one wants to believe we are victims of fate, so the universe aligns us in a way so that we mostly live life oblivious to the fact that there is a deeper meaning to everything about humanity. The lessons we agree to learn require circumstances to invoke the correct atmosphere, the perfect triggers, and at times enough power to draw us out right out of our comfort zone. Love in the human experience is a powerful propellant, creating uncontrollable needs and desires to ensure we use our inner strength to make changes. Love behaves as an amplified energy so strong that it is capable of creating scenes to nurture someone learning about stubbornness, violence, anger, hatred, jealousy, loyalty, obsession, guilt, joy, ecstasy, contentment, empathy, compassion, assertiveness, self-worth, confidence, communication and vulnerability.

Every relationship we encounter - lover, parental, friendship, colleagues, acquaintances - eventuate because are learning together and from each other. As discussed in Chapter Two, "First Love," I was not consciously aware of all of this, and the same was true at the time I met the tall man. Synchronicity ensured we collided; it is too unbelievable to be by chance, starting with the feeling that I belonged in Melbourne when I first went there eight years before the destined meeting. The suburb is where I ended up during and after my "love at first sight" interaction.

Melbourne is a city, with a population of almost five million. I did not meet him the first time I visited Melbourne during my soul-searching phase. I had to get to know myself, and felt driven to change my life, just as he had to bring a child into this world. In the second visit, synchronicity ensured the encounter with two girls who suggested the name of three bars; and when we tried to go to the bars, our efforts were thwarted and the other people in the line led me to the place where I met him.

You may be assuming I did this often, but I had never experienced a meeting like this before, despite being out thousands of times. I was extremely social, always was interacting with strangers, chatting, researching, dancing, and conversing; and I had never felt a connection with any man, nor been tempted by anyone in a social setting. I always felt my husband was perfect for me and I loved him. This was different - it came out of the blue and rocked my world. I might have been slow to understand the impact, but our meeting ensured I did not remain in my marriage, and more importantly, started the unravelling of my belief.

On a larger scale it prepared me first to gather the strength to finish what I already knew was troubled: my marriage, which I lived in each day feeling oppressed, while appearing to the world as wonderful. I did not even know that I was pretending, subconsciously, by not sharing my feelings or speaking about my teary nights home alone on the couch. No one knew because I did not tell them. I was told as a child to keep what goes on in the home to yourself and followed it through into adulthood and my own marriage.

The electricity that I physically felt on the first interaction with my tall man is something that I could not ignore. To this day I recall it. It ensured that I recognised his soul. Then, to increase the power of the bond and to ensure further attraction, I felt driven to seek him out to interact further.

As part of my human interest research I often asked random people questions to associate traits with astrological star signs.

Part of my criteria was the research of attraction: both superficially, across a crowded room; and connectively, with someone in your presence. I researched physical preference, emotional reaction and intimate sexual alignment. The tall man and his friend were no exception - both were barraged with my questions. When I posed one of my favourite sexual questions to the tall man, he responded with, "Yes." No one ever answered that question outright and I was delighted with his honest response, given that the question was an act I was intrigued with; another sign of compatibility for our fated union.

Sexual discussion is mostly shrouded in secrecy. The intimate nature of fantasies and desires make it difficult for many to express openly what they like (or actually do) in private. In the context of my research, a cautious response is fine as the two (or more) people involved in sexual acts are the only ones who really need to know detail.

Can you imagine meeting someone who has just become a parent and, being a mother yourself, continuing to see them? It is a battle of will, morals, many opinions in opposition to my emotions. My heart compelled me to keep seeing him while my will beat me up with the fear of judgement from those around me. I knew that I was being truthful with myself. I could not stop my involvement because I did not want to. The feeling of being with him was too good, all encompassing, passionate and easy, like nothing I had ever experienced. Apparently the feeling was mutual and the pull too strong for me to ignore.

My love at first sight meeting provided the beginning of the second major relationship in my life, the one that provided the personality traits of two people with background bruising who came together to learn hard lessons. I'll discuss my lessons and how I learned them in the next chapters. At this early stage, what I was experiencing was true love as the most intense, nurturing, beautiful encounters and deep heartfelt emotions I had ever felt or can accurately describe. In order to master communicating my feelings, to eventually behave differently to my previous relationship, this union took place to set up the perfect circumstances for me. Here was a second chance to behave differently, to be myself and to not slip back into self-oppression.

We never know at the time why, the answer only ever surfaces in hindsight; once the lesson is learned, the challenge overcome, only then does the purpose, the bigger picture of any experience, become clear.

Fate rules over free will.

Fate is absolute. This underlying serendipitous force brings people and circumstances together for us to experience life and to grow wiser, more empathetic, compassionate, tolerant and accepting of ourselves and others.

Life Actions

1. Can you think of any meeting that changed your perspective in a huge way?

2. Have you ever encountered someone that you felt an instant connection with?

3. Synchronicity ensures the life map transpires, when you begin to notice how it works you can see it weaving its way every day. Trust it.

**Connect with Toni and get
free resources to support you!**

www.ToniReillyInstitute.com/awake-bonus

CHAPTER 9:
SELF-AWARENESS, PAST LIVES
& REINCARNATION

My life map silently weaved its predestined course. At the age of thirty-six, when my marriage broke down, I became increasingly driven to find out about this psychic ability I supposedly possessed. At my next reading I inquired about my apparent abilities, asking how it was possible that I did not know I had these skills. The reader responded with a question. "When are you ever quiet?" I had never thought about it before, and on reflection, I answered truthfully with, "Only when I am asleep!" He told me that in order to embrace my sixth senses I needed to meditate. Meditation was the only way to slow down the mind and ease the distraction of life, allowing me to take notice of my innate sensory system. I was assured that my psychic ability would grow stronger as time passed.

I left that reading on a mission, fuelled by the intention of finding myself a meditation class. At that stage, I knew Buddhist monks meditated, so I assumed that was where I had to begin my search. Here I was, separated from my husband after 16 years; living in Brisbane, Queensland with my three children; and commuting interstate to Melbourne, Victoria every other week to spend time with my new love. This gave me seven days each fortnight to focus.

The Internet was already well established in the mid 2000's; however, spiritually-oriented sites lagged behind in digital technology, so selection was limited. As happened many times for me, a website randomly popped up in my browser belonging to a woman based in Melbourne, only a few kilometres away from where I was living. Her website looked reasonably normal - at least in comparison to my preconceived cliché notion of what psychics looked like, she did not fit. This woman appeared to be an everyday person with no signs of flowing gowns or crystal balls. Mary Malady listed meditation and psychic development classes so I emailed to express my interest; in response, she rang to tell me more about her teachings. I was beside myself with excitement and could not wait to attend. I invited my partner to come along with me but he was not interested, citing that it was "my thing."

Mary's classes facilitated profound personal shifts and provided life direction for me beyond anything I could have previously comprehended. To say they exceeded my expectations is an understatement. Classes were held weekly in Mary's lounge room, usually with eight girls. She had two classes a week, Monday evening and Wednesday morning. Given that I was only in Melbourne every other week, she let me crash both classes each fortnight. The very first time I sat in meditation I saw clairvoyantly. Clear images appeared in my mind; even though I did not understand them, I could see! They were not imagination. Instead, I saw random images in my mind. Here my clairvoyance was realised - in fact all of my extrasensory perceptions were stimulated. I continued with those classes for a couple of years. They were profound and they changed me.

In the early days, sitting in meditation twice during each class, I experienced prolific insight, visions and feelings which collectively spelled out insights to me about who I was. These insights highlighted my character, my fears, my shortcomings, my patterns, along with guidance to ensure I understood why I was being made aware of these attributes. I was waking up, becoming aware of our soul existence with self-awareness at the forefront. When I started those classes, I had not long before made the statement to my new partner that, "I do not have any issues." What!? Imagine my shock when, meditation after meditation, some other messed-up part of me would reveal itself and I realised I certainly did have issues, lots of them. Every class there was something else and I wondered how many issues there were.

I wrongly assumed because I had a nice childhood with functional parents that there was nothing wrong with me. As a matter of fact, I had never given any of this much thought. The fact that I had rarely given myself credit or taken notice of myself was a key pointer in many of my revelations.

Once, when I was paired with a much older woman in the morning class practicing psychic messages, our exercise was to tune to our partner and pass on what we picked up for them, she said, "You do not value yourself." I cried, not exactly knowing what it meant, but something about her statement resonated. During these classes it first occurred to me that being as passive as I was, especially in my relationships, stemmed from not valuing myself enough. Over more than nine years of reflection and self-development my answers revealed themselves, as did the triggers and reasons why this challenge was part of my life purpose.

Three years apart I was told the same thing during a reading with Jason. Twice he told me that Mary or Mary Ann was a good person who would be profound in my life. Well, I found Mary, years after being told of her in a reading, and she indeed profoundly impacted my life - and not just by teaching me to meditate and awaken my sixth senses. One evening during meditation class she suggested I read a book called *Many Lives Many Masters* by Dr. Brian Weiss. I did not ask what the book was about, instead I embarked on a focussed mission to buy a copy. It took me three weeks to find one, as this book was not considered mainstream, and the regular bookstores I searched in both Brisbane and Melbourne and they did not stock it. Three weeks later when I was in iconic Acland Street in St. Kilda, Melbourne, I went into Readings Bookstore where finally I found a copy. I purchased it, took it to a coffee shop a few doors down, and started reading. I soon discovered that the content was extraordinary, filled with concepts like nothing I had previously considered. It felt right, resonating with me at the core of my heart and soul. I read more than half the book before realising I had been in the café for several hours. I went home and finished the book that same evening.

Dr. Brian Weiss is a psychiatrist from the United States who shared his skepticism, discovery, and consequent convincing of the existence of reincarnation and past lives. The doctor's personal story unfolds when his patient recalled past-life memories causing an array of long-standing fears, phobias and behavioural patterns to clear for her, none of which had responded to years of traditional therapy. By recollecting memories from when his client had lived other lifetimes in various eras, cleared this young woman's problems with no side effects or use of drugs. It was simply miraculous with her issues being eliminated. I was in awe, at thirty-six years old, and for the first time I knew what I was here to do. At least for the time being. Regression formed a climactic piece of the jig-saw puzzle for meeting my destiny. My passion was ignited; the innate drive that ensued from this period changed my life forever. I became unstoppable, on a mission so focussed, my being was inspired. My guidance told me regression would be at the forefront for a time.

Prior to reading *Many Lives, Many Masters*, my exposure to past lives and reincarnation was limited to a reader stating that my son had been my father in a previous life. This information explained why my son bossed me around, even though he was a little boy. I understood how her statement weaved in, and it made sense. I wasn't skeptical of past lives; however, that was not the time for them to catch my attention.

The content within that book made me question a few of my own idiosyncrasies, ones I had disregarded or forgotten. It had never occurred to me that they were legitimate problems, nor had I entertained the concept that they could be fixed. I believed that one particular issue no longer held impact; in truth, it mattered more than ever before. In fact, I needed to fix three issues now, as they directly related to how my future was evolving.

Since Mary Malady told me to read the book, I assumed she must know someone who performed past life therapy. She did, so I booked in with her for past life regression the very next time I was in Melbourne. During my session I lay on her couch as she guided me into a relaxed state - then into a past life. In my mind's eye, almost like a vivid dream, I saw myself. I knew the nineteen-year-old girl in the old-fashioned dress was me. I felt it at my core and I sensed that this girl (Me) was as kind as kind could be.

Before regression I discussed with Mary the three issues I hoped to address. First: Why did I reach thirty-six years of age before becoming aware that I was psychic or had sixth senses? The second: Why did I go right through school covering my handwriting and later the computer screen so no one could read what I had written? My third issue: Why was I incapable of speaking in front of people? I don't even mean public speaking - if I was the centre of attention in front of my own family of five I would heat up from my feet right up to the top of my head, feeling as though I would faint. Believe me, I wanted to.

The first lifetime I recalled being a nineteen year-old-girl, in the U.S.A. I could see my father was a soldier in a blue coat; he was of importance in the army, working away for long periods of time. My mother had passed away giving birth to my 8-year-old brother. There was a lovely woman who came to our cottage to care for my brother and I. She had a large family of her own that she supported from her meagre wages earned as our housekeeper. I felt close to her; she was supportive of me, incredibly kind and loving to both my brother and me. I noted that the local people, mainly peasants, came to our cottage seeking me. We would sit together, opposite each other as I placed my hands over theirs, palm to palm, though not touching. I sensed strongly that somehow I raised hope, courage and strength with what I was able to tell them. Next I saw myself on a raised wooden platform, with people gathered around jeering and yelling, in the middle of main street of the town. I was about to be hung.

Somehow, someone assisted me to escape off the platform. I saw myself running out of town, where I sought refuge amongst some large rocks which formed a shelter where I died not long after from dehydration. On further investigation of that life, my little brother had innocently mentioned to a friend what I did with the people using my hands. That boy told his parents and consequently the authorities came to get me and to kill me, ignorant and afraid of what I did.

It made sense that perhaps I feared using my intuitive abilities now, as subconsciously I remembered the mis-understanding, hatred and even my death. After that regression my intuitive senses in current life intensified in strength and I was confident using them.

During my first regression session, Mary guided me to a second past life. This time I was a man, robust around the girth and wearing a red coat with white stockings, black knee length tight pants with black buckled shoes, and a wig, curled up under my hat. I saw through a window facing the narrow main street that I was writing with a quill. I wrote exquisitely, in a large hardcover leather-bound book, which was positioned on a stand, rather like a lectern. I felt that I was the mayor, or at least well-respected in my town. In the next scene I saw myself in the doorway in the front of the window with many local people gathered around for a town meeting, which I had called. Apparently I was warning them of a storm, which I had foreseen, which would cause major damage to their homes and our town. They demanded to know how I knew. The people began to question how I knew of this pending storm. Deciding I was mad or a crook, they took no notice of my advice. Instead of preparing for the natural disaster, they turned on me and I was imprisoned, deemed to have gone mad. People searched my office and discovered my journals filled with prophetic insights. I was never freed, dying years later all alone in a cell.

This recollection cleared my fear of people reading anything written by me and relieved my fear of speaking in front of people. I was able to attend a short course in public speaking which my friend Shawnee attended with me.

For the first time it became easy to write. This occurred in synchronistic timing, opening the way to begin speaking about regression. Now I was able to prepare website content, social media postings, and advertisements, as well as share my thoughts in articles and hound various media to publish them. I confidently kept notes and provided email guidance for my clients. As I developed, my research diverted towards emotional suffering along with the physical effects it manifested. I went on to produce intensive course content, a self-help book, cards and meditations while regularly contributing articles for publication, print, digital media, various blogs and news sites.

Speaking in front of people came easily. I went from feeling I would faint to barely being able to contain my content within the allocated timeframe at events. I started meditation classes for small to medium groups and presented seminars and self-healing workshops in front of hundreds of people.

Without logical explanation, I was aware that past life regression would play an integral role in my life for a time. Mary

Malady trained me, and as it turned out, I was a natural - confidently facilitating past life regression for those who sought it, usually achieving outstanding results. I don't even know where all my clients came from, but they showed up in abundance; clearly they were universally sent. I was guided in various meditations to keep notes of the session for future reference. Occasionally a client shared messages directly for me, many times I learned from them as they were healed in the process. People came in droves to assist during my apprenticeship to understand human nature and my subsequent evolution into a pioneering practitioner.

After about a year of facilitating past life regression for clients, I felt it was important to train with Dr. Brian Weiss. He taught an annual course for therapists in Rhinebeck, New York. By this stage, I was hosting a fortnightly meditation group in Brisbane while attending Mary's classes when in Melbourne. One evening a couple of weeks prior to my trip to New York to train under Dr. Brian Weiss, I heard a loud voice during meditation saying, "You're going to meet a teacher over there." I was smug responding with, "I know, his name is Brian!" Imagine my surprise when I heard, "His name is Dan, Dan and Dave, Dan and Dave, Dan and Dave." I was still learning to discern my thoughts from messages of guidance; you see, they come in as thoughts. Even still, this was so clear that I shared what was said with the fifteen or so people sitting in my group that evening. I'd put it out there - only time would tell if I had received legitimate insight pertaining to my life.

In New York City I made my way to Port Authority Bus Terminal to ride to Omega campus, which was about two hours' drive north to begin my course. Being a tourist I sat at the front of the bus for a clear view of the road so I could enjoy the landscape. The coach filled with people, all heading to Omega campus. No one sat next to me, leaving the seat beside mine the last vacant one. When a man asked if he could sit there, I said, "Of course." We introduced ourselves. His name was Dan! We talked the entire road trip and our conversation flowed easily. We both felt at ease - it was as if I already knew this person whom I had only just met. Dan is a hypnotherapist, with an analytical mind, soft heart, and a challenging personal story. His introduction to the energetic realms was when he asked what I did for a living.

Sure enough, when were allocated accommodation on campus, Dan's roommate was a man named Dave. All three of us were there to participate in Past Life Regression Training; all three of us were taken into the course at the last minute from the wait list. We spent most of our free time discussing life and our lives, and our conversation flowed freely. I was excited to find a man who was skeptical, but at least open to my claims of how energy worked. At that time, pendulums fascinated me so I took Dan to the campus store to find one so I could show him how they work. We found them in the middle of the store, about fifteen or so hanging together on display. When I walked near them they swayed back and forth. Dan checked for a breeze, an open door or other people, but there was nothing to cause this. He was incredulous that these pendulums were moving purely from my energy.

Synchronicity took over, assuring that teachers, mentors, like minds, and support came to me at an incredible pace. I noticed it happening everywhere, unplanned, unexpected, and often bordering on miraculous. The number 36 is a sign for me, ever since I was seven years old and won a jar of lollies when I guessed the correct quantity of 236. Directly above where I sat in the large training hall next to Dan there was the number 36 printed on a light. I took it as assurance, confident that I was perfectly positioned in my life.

Following the breakdown of my marriage, which was the turning point in my life, my universal assignment was to grow familiar with myself. It proved to be my time to delve deeper into (among other things) my tendency to be submissive with a partner, compromising to my own detriment. I consciously declared it a priority not to fall into the same oppressive pattern in my new relationship - and to ensure I was successful, I stated my objective to him. Over time I repeatedly offended, only this time it was different. I found it easier to say what I wanted and to be myself, even though it was extremely challenging at times. I usually had to work up the courage before I could state my case. It took eight years and many scenarios before I realised I had attracted a partner who was a mirror of myself. He was so similar to me, a serial people-pleaser; and while my challenges were with men, his were with women.

The challenges I was destined to overcome through this

relationship provoked deep intense emotions, nothing like I had experienced previously. It was as though we were in some sort of contest designed to prove individual personal worthiness to ourselves. This relationship paved the way, providing many occasions where I was forced to communicate with him, to bare my soul by being completely vulnerable.

My tendency to keep the peace by carefully orchestrating my responses to avoid judgement had taken its toll. Inner tension and bitterness had brewed and festered over many years, so an outburst to release this energy was inevitable. Now I was defensive; I guarded my new-found self-expression by defending myself relentlessly, and he was on the end of it.

As hard as I tried not to, I still fell into my passive ways, though never to the same extent as in my marriage. I repeated some things again because as I was not aware of the cause and I did not understand why I reacted in the way that I did. The silent treatment is emotional torture, and in my new relationship, I vowed I would not allow this again. I believed I could control myself but still I withdrew, at least long enough to work out how to express my feelings.

My first test arrived after my new man left his long-term relationship and, with my encouragement, assumed shared care of his young child. At that stage, the arrangement for my three children was 50/50: one week with me, then one week with their father, in a continuous rotation. This worked extremely well for me, my children and their father (as logistically, we lived one suburb apart) so there was no drastic change or distance for us to navigate.

This arrangement initially and inadvertently ensured I recouped some time to myself. I had been a 24/7 mother for the past ten years. These seven days on my own every other week were bliss. I knew other Mums in a similar situation who cried when the children went to their father for his week. Not me! My kids never complained about going to their Dad's, so I had no guilt about relishing this precious time to myself. The week passed by quickly, and before I knew it, we were together again.

My passion was ignited, making my ambition relentless. So I directed my energy into establishing a reputable therapeutic practice and an esteemed profile. For the first time since school, I had the notion, as well as time, to study, write and approach the media to publish my articles.

I travelled abroad to attend courses while flying five hours roundtrip interstate to be with my new love every second Friday. Our personal circumstances were tricky, to say the least. Being based in two different states; he, father to a small child; and me, the mother to three young children. It was never going to be easy. Despite the long distances, I was deliriously happy seeing my man every other week, feeling liberated to have recovered my freedom. I was able to establish friendships, develop as a person, and study while nurturing my children, all without the distraction or expectation of a live-in partner.

I worked part-time at FireWorks Gallery (a modern Aboriginal art gallery in Brisbane) and I needed to make up time for the week I was interstate to ensure that the week with my kids was full. I adored being with them on my light-hearted terms. We had fun together, and all four of us helped with the running of our home. I was used to being the main carer of our family; so from my perspective, no husband or partner meant I had one less person to consider and take care of. I devoured parenting minus the opinion of another parent. While married I parented to my husband's insecurities and paranoia, not my laid- back, fuss-free, easygoing way. I promoted independence, not control. I wanted more than anything for my kids to feel as though they could be themselves, to nurture what they aspired to, while also embracing their innate traits. It was important to me that they were confident in using their own radar, independent of mine, at ease following their life plan.

In contrast, my former husband was a worrier, telling me how to prepare for potential falls, or accidents. Living up to the expectations of someone else was stressful. Being free of the pressure following our spilt and parenting in my own liberal but effective way was bliss. Not long into my personal emancipation I was faced with protecting it. I refused to relinquish my newly claimed chance to focus on my dreams - it simply was not an option.

My first challenge to communicate assertively presented itself around care for my new partner's daughter. Her mother travelled for work so it made sense for her father to take care of her. I travelled interstate to be together every second week when my children were with their father. I was working for an employer in my state, and I wanted to devote this time to building my dream while my days were free of mainstream employment. I worked productively at home while he went to work each day. I put that aside to take care of his toddler when these situations arose. She was easy to care for; still, I did not want to be tied to caring for a small child - I had just finished that phase with my own three children. I relished this time to firmly establish my career. Caring for a toddler all day was out of the question. My own children went to childcare when I worked and I felt this was a reasonable option for my partner's child.

In the lead up to declaring that I wanted to spend business hours dedicating time to my business, I experienced anxiety for the first time. I would wake in the middle of the night to a crushing feeling in my chest so intense that I felt pinned to the bed. It took me a few nights to realise that it was my body telling me that I had to talk to my partner to let him know that I did not want to take care of a toddler during the day. I eventually gathered the courage to talk to him, explaining how over the past ten years since I'd had children there had been limited time to myself. I shared with him how important it was to me to use this time for myself now.

I hesitated to have the discussion, feeling certain I would offend him. My worst fear came true. When I finally raised the situation, he said he understood; but truthfully, he was not able to relate, having his first child at forty, and prior to becoming a father, owning the luxury of twenty-four hours a day to do whatever he chose, with no children to demand his attention or be responsible for. His accomplishments came before children, as a successful high-profile elite athlete, earning two degrees while establishing himself in his chosen career.

Unfortunately he took my request personally, perceiving my wishes to keep the daytime free to focus on my passion, to establish solid foundations working on my purpose, as me not wanting anything to do with his child. That was never what I said, nor was it what I meant. The misinterpretation caused me to spend the next few months explaining over and over in an futile attempt to make him understand. Unfortunately his interpretation was rock solid, I was unable to sway his already set perception, so eventually I gave up trying to break through. I had to accept that I failed to convince him of my true intentions. I loathed being resented. It frustrated me that he did not listen, seeming incapable of comprehending what I actually said. I defended myself until I could do it no longer. Finally I surrendered. Feeling defeated, I returned to Queensland.

We are volunteers, not victims.

When a certain purpose is part of your life map, compulsion takes over to follow through. Nothing that is meant to be yours will ever pass you by, whether a fated meeting, opportunity, job or relationship.

If you are waiting for your Mr. or Ms. Right to come along, the best thing you can do is have faith that they will arrive as planned in the universal timing - not according to your free will. You may as well relax and enjoy other things in life until then!

Life Actions

1. Do you have a checklist of expectations for a partner? Are they realistic?

2. Have you met someone special who was nothing like your usual type?

3. Have you ever experienced a connection and felt immediately challenged by them – in a good way?

**Connect with Toni and get
free resources to support you!**

www.ToniReillyInstitute.com/awake-bonus

CHAPTER 10:
EDUCATION, INTELLECT & WISDOM

When I was in my twenties I felt inferior, somehow not up to scratch. I blamed leaving school early and my lack of formal education for the absence of sophisticated vocabulary as well as for my inability to engage in conversation about politics or economics. It never occurred to me that partaking in conversation which did not spark my interest was nothing to do with formal education; I simply did not resonate with these topics, and I still don't. The difference is that now I am comfortable admitting my disinterest, withdrawing or listening on the sidelines. As an adult, I attended (amongst others) a renowned college for intuitive studies in England, a course in New York, as well as my most profound training course, held in Melbourne - just two days in the teachers' lounge room. I've embraced a completely different perspective of my own intellect, as well as discerning between education and wisdom. I attribute knowledge to life gathered through experience, which is passed on by others. Knowledge passed on from other people's research is defined and presented through a perspective filtered by their individual value and belief system.

I surmised that life experience, combined with intellectual capacity gained through past lives and the intelligence stored in our soul energy, provides the ultimate qualification of wisdom. I earned my knowledge through years of employment, working hands on in many varied positions. My jobs started out basic, ensuring my earning capacity was standard minimum wage. It turns out that my work choices were exactly what I needed to develop professional skills as well as practical application of the necessary tools to run a successful business while developing communication skills. I acquired the ability to navigate my way through the digital age. Life experience awarded me significant knowledge which, when combined with innate wisdom, inspired me to share my philosophy with others.

I concede that a kind heart, with the critical understanding that all people are similar at the core, innately knowing that we are emotional beings experiencing our way through life, doing the best we can with what we know, forms the basis for my wisdom. I have witnessed people speak loudly of their profound insights who could be viewed as dysfunctional; and I've seen others who are highly educated, or academic, with little wisdom or common sense. Every position I worked in taught me something. Many times I was given knowledge at the core level without having to undertake arduous study, I was granted the opportunity to learn various practical, technical and graphic skills by default, inadvertently shared by the ones I worked with. This is my preferred way to learn.

I never went to university, yet I did attend various courses and further education classes over the years, all around the world. This helps me to reach my potential while allowing me to fully realise my purpose. Of course I always *was* living out my purpose; it was my human side that questioned my education (or lack of) as I saw it.

My most profound influential teachings of all were earned through personal challenges. My colleagues and peers in roles above my status in the chain of command all attributed to my growth, while I learned about my strengths and challenges through my personal love relationships - both in their glory and during their demise. The personalities of my children, traits of friends, as well as their experiences of which I was privy to in intimate detail, and the many ups and downs of people close to me, showed me about life.

My degree in the coaching of life was earned firsthand by working with people. My many clients taught me about humanity and why we are. People-watching, observing behaviour and research by talking to people, are in my opinion the most valuable training I underwent. I used to believe people (including myself) were complex: an enigma, unable to be fully understood, and continually open to misinterpretation or misdiagnosis. I discovered this is not true, that we are not tremendously different to each other.

Visible differences in appearance, status, background, culture, wealth, poverty, gender, sexual orientation or personal experiences or physical health do not make us different at the core. These aspects merely provide varying circumstances and means to master the same few things that humans come to earth to learn in what I call the School of Life.

Inhabiting a body allows us to experience senses, which are not available to us in our energetic form. Taste, touch, sight, smell, feelings and emotions are the gems available for enjoyment or endurance while we are here. These are the treasures of our existence.

We all have feelings, making us the same, no matter how we appear or what we are raised to believe. They are key drivers throughout life. We are here to learn about emotion. Life is the university where our soul can experience emotion, which can never be learned via a textbook or lecture or even another person telling us about their feelings. Emotions have to be felt, facilitated by an experience, unique to each individual. It is the only legitimate way. Real life presents circumstances for us to get in touch with our feelings, while our natural reaction is to oppress them; or in vulnerability, to reveal them.

Our soul plans for each incarnation on earth, ensuring that we are born with a specific personality, complete with a pre-determined individual set of traits that have been carefully selected, with the aim of assisting our learning throughout our lifetime. The journey is individual, however other souls are required to help us to learn; their job is to trigger emotional reactions which create a shake-up at the depth of our being. In simple terms, others assist by invoking feelings of deep love for someone - a parent, partner, child, or pet; or envy, anger, frustration, disappointment, and guilt, with the long list of emotions and behaviours we are capable of inflicting and acting out. No emotions are bad; they are simply the underlying purpose to our lives. Individually, we attempt to hide our feelings or overly display them; often, we will do both during incarnation.

I developed a deep respect for life, humanity and a fearless peace with death.

In 1984, I completed my high school studies at the age of 14. I had no intention to continue to senior level; school was never my favourite place. To fit in, I had to be quiet, so I zoned out most of the time and daydreamed my way through school. I've pondered how anything sunk in, wondering how I could possibly have taken the information in when I barely listened. Fortunately, it stockpiled in my subconscious memory. I managed to be an above-average student. The day I left school was the beginning of a liberating time for me. My confidence boomed, fuelled by my desire to be independent and grown-up.

Despite insecurities around my lack of formal further education due to leaving school at such a young age, nothing hindered my progress in life. I was naturally determined and generally had healthy self-esteem when it came to work.

At 15, I joined the workforce full-time as a bakery assistant. At that time I never envisaged how tremendous my life would become. I enjoyed the responsibility that work entitled me; the thing I favoured most was interacting with customers. I was bubbly, with a warm smile and I always felt genuinely pleased to see them. I was left in charge of the store from early morning, when the baker left, right up until to closing the premises at the end of business each day. I was in my element - in charge of myself, being responsible by nature, I thrived without the oppression of being bossed around.

As part of my progress into the workforce, no longer a student studying at school, another brilliant scenario evolved when I was treated as an adult by my family. I was allowed to make my own decisions with their support and guidance. Being a responsible girl, unrestricted by dictator parents, I had no need to rebel or keep secrets from my them; I shared all that happened in my life with my Mum.

During my teenage years I became interested in ghosts. I liked to watch horror movies and read ghost stories. Though it never occurred to me that ghosts or spirits were real, they fascinated me. My off-handed approach to ghosts changed the day my Mum told me about an encounter she had in our house when I was 7 years old.

When my family returned from an extended holiday exploring

Australia, we moved into a house that my parents owned and rented out. The house was on John Street, Cowra - a town in the Central West region of New South Wales, Australia, 310 kilometers (193 miles) southwest of Sydney. Mum mentioned that the lady who rented the house before we moved in had told of hearing footsteps going in the house - along with other strange things. I listened in awe as she described her own encounters there when our family moved in. Like the internal sliding door from the hall to the living room opening inwards, seemingly pushed, and the sound of footsteps walking down the carpeted hall and out the locked front door. I heard the sound of knocking on the door outside my bedroom, which led to a balcony with no one on it. Mum described other things that happened in that house, though there was never anyone there (at least not physically). I was sold - if my Mum said it, she only ever told the truth. In my eyes, my mother epitomised honesty. Mum was not afraid, either; she told the story so matter-of-fact, as though these were ordinary occurrences, like any other story of the day. She did not get caught up in any fear or spookiness around hauntings. When I asked if she was afraid, she said they did nothing to her, and surely they would have, if they were here to cause harm.

In retrospect, I have believed in U.F.O.'s (unidentified flying objects) since I was little. My family used to watch a television show in the 1970s when I was six, and those cases intrigued me. I felt that it was impossible that we human beings were "it" - I have always felt strongly that we as a human race were arrogant to think that *we* were all that existed. It made no sense to me, even with my limited knowledge of astronomy, science or the human psyche that we could be the only living beings. That earth was the only planet with life existing did not add up; it simply was not feasible in my mind. Years later my mother shared a story of seeing a spaceship-type aircraft, assuring my inner knowing. Life on other planets is not where my interest and research was directed; I believe those existences are schools, like earth, where souls experience different things. Many people have shared their encounters, and they are far too many for me to cast them aside as mad or fanciful.

None of it really mattered, as I was way too busy being a teenager to be giving thought to spirits; but those stories served their purpose, morphing their way into my belief system for reference many years later.

In my teenage years, I lived with my family in a small mining town called Glenden in Queensland, Australia, a twelve-hour drive from Brisbane, boasting a population of 1500. Everybody knew everyone. That small community energy facilitated great freedom, as by default people looked out for each other, and the safety of that community worked very well for my personality. At that stage attending university was out of the question, as it meant not working or earning money; besides, I wanted to be a hairdresser, and there was no need to go to university for that!

My life was fun - I was busy, rarely distracted with anything more than what I was doing next with my friends or what I would wear when I went out. Weekends were filled with trips to coastal beaches, inland water holes, camping or occasionally staying in resorts. There was always a group of us hanging out together. If we were not going away for the weekend our time was spent water skiing at the lake or attending bar-b-ques infused with dancing and never-ending conversation. That was what my life was all about, and I loved it.

I was never great with managing money, and as soon as I earned it, I spent every cent on clothes or going out. I often had something new to wear on the weekends. I loved clothes; I was either buying or sewing them. I thrived on creating clothes, and sometimes I created my own designs. I spent my free time sewing, sometimes with a pattern and other times freehand. I was forever collecting fabric to experiment with. I would see a dress or outfit in a magazine and attempt to copy it; occasionally I was successful, though there were plenty of disasters, outfits which never made it, and there were many creations which I only ever wore once.

When I was 17, I left Glenden and moved into a flat in the nearest larger town called Mackay on the coast of North Queensland, as I had found myself a job at the local paper, *The Daily Mercury*. I was always smiling while carrying out my less - than-challenging gopher duties; I felt happy though, as I was surrounded by people - lots of them. It turned out that I was a bit too noisy, as I was always friendly to the customers (this is the place I mentioned earlier, where I was reprimanded for being too loud by the woman who managed the office). That working environment was stifling, filled with women from 16 to 60, many of whom had been working there all of their lives, starting there as their first job after they had finished school. I could barely comprehend having the same workplace for a lifetime. It was apparent to me that many of these women were stuck in a rut - afraid to smile or be jovial at work, or perhaps they did not entertain the notion that life did not need to be so serious. The energy of that office environment dampened my spirit. I couldn't stay there, being watched and told how to behave, to withhold my joyful personality in case I upset the oppressed unhappy manager. On my office rounds, delivering mail and memorandums, I discovered that another department needed a girl. I went to work there, where my personality was appreciated and used to advantage.

As synchronicity would have it, although I was totally unaware, there was a man who used to drive me to the post office every afternoon. His name was Glen. Being 17, I thought he was old; I'd guess he was about 60 years. He was kind, and we talked every day on the drive. Glen had one of his fingertips missing. One day I asked him what had happened, and he told me he cut it off with a meat saw when he worked as a butcher in his younger years. When I told the other young girls they were horrified that I had asked him.

A friendship developed with Glen. He liked my bright personality; because of it, he told me about the hotel he drank at each afternoon, where he thought I would make a good bar attendant. He enquired about me working there, so from the age of 18, I went to work at the hotel by night and the newspaper by day. I enjoyed working in the bar - it was exhilarating, interacting with the regular patrons who came each weekday afternoon for their set consumption of beer and daily catch-up with the others who did the same thing before going home for the evening.

I decided that the bar work suited me better than the semi-oppressive environment at the newspaper, so I started at another hotel to work solely as a bar attendant. I worked until 2 a.m. on weekend nights in a lounge bar with a live musician. I was always efficient, mostly running the bar on my own.

One morning when I was 19, I was called to work unexpectedly at short notice. I was an extremely responsible person; I always showed up for work, or would go immediately if I was asked, because never letting anyone down was important to me. On arrival I was surprised to learn I was not called in to work; instead, I was directed to an area of the hotel that I never knew existed to be interviewed by police. Apparently some money had gone missing from the office.

The detectives interviewed me. They were undermining and disrespectful, planting suggestions and scenarios for why I would steal money. They asked about the car which I had recently taken my first loan to buy. They insinuated I could use extra money to put towards that. I could not contain my fury, unable to hide the anger I was feeling, as was evident in my tone. I had never even been near the office where the money was missing from; in fact I had never even been upstairs in the hotel until this interview. I was furious that they were treating me like a dishonest thief. For a rare moment I was overwhelmed with anger, which I kept down for fear of behaving badly. *How dare they wrongfully accuse me?!*

I was very sensitive, taking the whole thing personally. I left the hotel after that interview, indignant and devastated. I cried hysterically while trying to rationalize that they must investigate all possibilities.

I did not stay working at that hotel. I couldn't; my pride was hurt and I was angry at them questioning me. I went back to where I originally started bartending at Taylors Hotel, which was under new management. I was happy, as I had some day shifts; most of the shifts in bar work are at night, so it was a nice change to have a mix of shift times. My return to that hotel was short lived, though; I developed a rash on my fingers. It was eczema, on my left hand, and it was itchy and looked gross. The doctor gave me cortisone to settle it down and said that the beer making contact with my skin was the cause of it. When I told my boss, he promptly dismissed me! That freaked me out. Losing my job was not something I saw coming. I did not know how I would earn money - it felt like my world had fallen apart!

Even when events seem tragic or take us by surprise, they are creating an opportunity. The circumstances often present as an issue that seems insurmountable at the time and catches us off-guard. By being thrown out of our comfort zone we are forced to rise to the challenge, which is presented as a chance to change. Change is always for the better. This crash presented an incredible thrust in a new direction. Apparently there were other skills for me to learn, along with a new phase in my life to navigate.

My best friend Ness was working with a construction company out near Glenden. She asked her boss if I could work there - which meant, suddenly, I had an administration job in the office at the remote site. Sight unseen, no interview, no phone call, I just had to show up for work Monday.

I was nineteen and it was 1990. I had very little experience with computers, and the revolutionary Microsoft Windows was a new phenomenon. On my first day, the General Manager asked me to type a memorandum. There I was, the only person in the office, sitting at a computer, looking at a new document open in this program called "Word" with no idea how to start typing or even how to use a mouse! Lucky for me, in the next office was a young engineer, fresh out of university, who showed me how to click the mouse. Talk about thrown in the deep end, leaving me no choice but to swim! I swam, discovering that computers came easily to me. Soon I was helping the other girls with tips and tricks. Apparently I had a natural flair with technology.

The construction project where I worked was full-on in many ways. The site location was remote, with no accommodation there for women; so all the girls in the office (including me) lived in the nearest town. An engineer who also lived in town picked us up each morning for the forty-minute drive to the worksite to begin our ten hour shift. There was a deadline to meet; the days were long, and we were kept on our toes. I lived with my parents, so it was easy for me, compared to the others. I would get home to dinner which Mum had prepared, while the others made meals for their partners and kept house as well. Those days were relentless - consumed by work, returning home in time to catch some sleep, only to repeat the commute and work day all over again.

The exception was having a social drink after work. Being very social, we were always up for a long conversation, often arriving home for an hour or two of sleep. There were times, after a boozy night out, when I was not very productive on the job. We managed to secure a vehicle and occasionally a driver to take us forty-five minutes to the nearest town on dirt roads to buy hangover food. They were fun times.

I was secretary to an engineer whose job was to produce the company health and safety procedure manual. I touch-typed his handwritten notes at great speed.

When construction of the coal mine was complete it led on to an administration job for me as a receptionist at the company's head office in Mackay. Mackay is a small city; however, after spending time in Glenden on the remote construction site, it seemed huge. It was a nice change to be somewhere with shops, nightclubs and restaurants. I enjoyed my new job, always left to my own devices to complete tasks. Some of my colleagues were social after work, which was a bonus.

When I was 22, a South African man came to the office for a meeting. As he passed me on the reception desk, he approached to offer me a job. I was flattered. The thought of being the only office person for the new workshop he was setting up was appealing. I was hired slightly prematurely though, as initially it was just him and me for a couple of weeks. There was nothing much for me to do while the workshop and office were being constructed. For that period, I regretted leaving my fun reception job at the mine office. It did not take long for the business to power on full-steam ahead - there was a new office to fit out with furniture, computers, plus a large workshop which required equipment and tradesmen to carry out maintenance on specialty underground mining machinery.

We needed sales staff, onsite fitters, electricians, and administration - all had to be set up for the thriving leg of an already-established international company. My boss knew how to write software to manage our administration records, timesheets and job costing. As it was my job to enter all the data, I regularly asked him to modify the software to make the process easier. When he was programing, I looked over his shoulder and soon I took over programming our software; that is how my affiliation with computer programming began.

I learned so much that I was allowed to own my job, which I carried out with little or no direction. This worked well with my determined, capable traits and my yearning for the freedom to use my brain. What I learned on the job far outweighs what I could have learned through a textbook. It suited me best to learn by hands-on experience.

Interacting with people was easy for me. I was efficient; if I did not know what to do I could easily devise a solution. My administration and office management positions not only taught me practical skills, they allowed me a platform to study the coaching of people, as well as gain insight into men. The predominant energy around me was masculine, as my colleagues, peers and superiors were men. My professional, efficient, friendly interaction remained untainted, as I never altered it by sleeping with any of my colleagues. Seducing anyone was the last thing on my mind. Manipulating men to get ahead in my working environment, or personally, was not part of my role in this life. I could see when this type of interaction was developing or happening between two people, and sometimes I was privy to knowing directly about clandestine affairs. I felt at ease being trusted with secrets, as I am by nature a vault when granted the honour of insights into the psyche, deepest fears and secret behaviours of others. I have always believed that there is no stopping a fated connection, so I never judged. I learned that the connections shared between people are not always supposed to lead to a fanciful future together; I realized that these interactions come about to serve the purpose of learning many things in life. They are not always sexual; some connections occur to escalate strength, courage or tolerance by providing support or challenges which force people to stand up for themselves. Some affairs take a curvy path, others become major love relationships.

That period was the end of working with only myself to consider, as I married at 24; then at 25, I became a mother. My work transpired into an attempt at a fashion label for toddlers and babies. I sewed hundreds of outfits, which I sold to a few local boutiques, adorned with my professionally embroidered label.

I was planning to be a stay at home Mum but the reality was far less fulfilling than I anticipated. When my first baby was 4 months old I returned to my office job for one day a week. Something was different; I had changed, and though I welcomed interaction outside of home and relished adult conversation, certain things that seemed important before were not anymore, now that I had a child to care for. The stresses and insecurities of my colleagues seemed unnecessarily dramatic, reducing my tolerance for little things being blown out of proportion.

When I was 27 my husband and two children relocated to Brisbane, a much larger city. I became a mother to three children while continuing to work in various administration roles. Each position taught me how different industries operate and I acquired many business skills. My interest turned towards observing dynamics of the people I worked amongst.

In my late 20s, my husband's sister (whom I was close to) married a gorgeous artist who owned an aboriginal art gallery in Brisbane. Soon I began working there, first producing software to manage their inventory, then as a gallery assistant. My sister-in-law was an interior and graphic designer, and we worked together to produce beautiful in-depth catalogues showcasing artists the gallery represented, as well as advertising material. I learned about visual placement and I began to comprehend appreciation of beauty in things I had never even noticed, let alone been able to admire. I recognised intricate attributes that alter perception, at least from a visual perspective. She had an eye for detail like no one else. Working with her is a blessing for which I will forever remain grateful. I worked at the gallery for six years, and it was my final position as an employee. My degree in the practicalities of business, behind the scenes on that level, was complete.

I had undertaken measures to build a public profile for myself and was passionately following my purpose of working with people. I felt compelled to continue in the direction of making a difference with people's emotions by providing affirmation and guidance so that they were at ease with themselves and confident to enter the next phase in their lives.

Working for others not only taught me many practical skills, but also helped me become proficient with the skills needed to work for myself. I view those years as my degree. The paradox of being surrounded by people and loving to interact with them was overshadowed by my strong desire to independently create without the obstruction of restricting corporate rules, hierarchy or office politics. Creativity is aligned with intuition, and for it to flow, I must be alone - so being my own boss granted me the right circumstances to live to my innate traits. Even the contradiction of my introvert and extrovert qualities are used to their fullest potential, given the material and programs I create a present to many people.

Knowledge is human; Wisdom is soul.

Knowledge is learned through retaining information presented by another person; Intellect is the capacity to perceive information. Wisdom is philosophy or streamed insight from your soul energy or based on observation and experiential experiences.

Life Actions

1. Do you associate more as a creative or logical person?

2. Would you like to actively access your soul wisdom?

3. Are you keen to strengthen your intuitive stream?

**Connect with Toni and get
free resources to support you!**

www.ToniReillyInstitute.com/awake-bonus

CHAPTER 11:
YOUR BODY IMAGE

Where do concerns about our physical appearance stem from? How do they perpetuate into insecurities that are capable of consuming our everyday thoughts? Why do we form distorted perceptions of our body and where do these ideas about ourselves come from? I personally do not blame magazines, television or social media for my body consciousness, as these influences were not readily available to me in the era or environment that I was raised in. My hang-ups took hold through offhanded remarks, mentioned flippantly, festered by my own harsh self-critiquing while comparing myself to others.

This chapter highlights a paradox in my life. Nudity in my home, when I was growing up, was casual and acceptable; still, this liberal approach, neither sleazy nor "out there", did not stop me from developing body image issues. My family home only ever had one bathroom, and it was shared by all five of us. I streaked from the bathroom, and if I had forgotten a towel, my sister and I never thought twice about barging in on each other. With my Mum, there was never a question of knocking, it was always O.K. to come in unannounced. So being comfortable with my body was inadvertently instilled in my home, ensuring a feeling of ease while naked. The lack of critical observation of my shape fostered a healthy body image for me. I carried that confidently into my sexual relationships and later, in my family home with my children.

I consider my overall body image to be healthy. Never hiding my body in relationships, I am relaxed with nudity. I once had a brief conversation with a mother of two young girls when I was collecting my children from child care, and her story alarmed me. She said, "You know, when you have a shower with the kids with your t-shirt on..." I did not respond. I listened, but no - I had never showered or bathed myself or my kids in clothes. In our home we bathed naked, even if it was together; in fact, my kids took great delight in hitting my butt, then laughing hysterically at it wobbling. I wondered how her girls' body image would be impacted in the future by the way their mother was passing on her own body issues.

Our soul comes here to experience all sorts of things. We choose our parents and they choose their children. Even though I was alarmed at this Mother's off-handed story, her children will have come here (to Earth) knowing, on a soul-level at least, that this is something to learn about. Later in life it is likely that they will be challenged to overcome any effects, as will their mother. What happened to this woman to make her believe that she should not be naked with her own children? Her beliefs are passed down as paranoia or concern, which progresses to affect her children - though this only occurs if their souls are meant to be affected. Can you see how "normal" is defined by the ideals we are raised with, whatever they may be?

I was an average-sized child, pretty much the same as all the other children of similar age. Overweight children were virtually non-existent when I started school in the mid 70s. I didn't pay any attention to my appearance until I was five years old. During my first year of school the little girls in my class refused to play with me. In an attempt to comprehend why, I compared myself physically to them. Whilst trying to find reasons why they did not like me, I became conscious of my appearance. I looked at those little girls who did not want to play with me and thought to myself, "If I had skin that colour, maybe they would like me." Or, "If I had hair like her, maybe she would play with me." At that young age I lacked any understanding of emotional expression, and certainly had no knowledge of a bigger life plan, or that there was a purpose to being excluded by them.

One afternoon after school when I was about six, my sister and I were in the bedroom that we shared with Mum, who was sitting on my sister's bed, folding clothes. My sister and I were hanging up our school uniforms when Mum made an innocent comparison about my bum being a different shape than my sister.

Even though it was a legitimate and accurate observation, given that my sister had a different body shape to me, I didn't have the capability to see myself from behind to notice my actual size, nor did I comprehend that we were simply different shapes. From that moment on I was convinced that I had a big bum. I envisaged it as extremely out of proportion, and my warped perception stayed with me until I was 30. It seems ridiculous in hindsight that an innocent comment could affect me for 25 years, but it did.

I was interested in fashion, always carefully selecting clothing to cover my bum. I usually chose A-line dresses and long tops; in the summer, I covered my bikini in a t-shirt to hide my shape.

Another body image issue arose when I reached puberty. Nothing much was happening in my bust area; I had noticed that my sister developed breasts and I wanted some too! By the time I was 14, there was no indication that I would need a bra anytime soon. That was traumatic for me, as all the girls at school wore them, and I knew this because they were visible through the white blouse of our uniform. My best friend, who incidentally had an extra-large set of breasts, assured me that mine would grow. She often patiently reminded me that her sister did not have any at fourteen - but they grew later when she was seventeen. She reassured me that there was hope; so, I lived in hope.

My breasts never grew beyond an AA size, only ever managing to fit into a trainer bra; so I was left with little choice but to accept that this was all I was getting. The whole issue shifted into the background of my thoughts as I became focussed on other important things in my life at the time.

I inherited my small breasts from Mum; we used to laugh about it, agreeing wholeheartedly how unfair it was to end up with no boobs when there were girls who were blessed with our share as well as their own. Looking for reasons to explain what nature had given us, we would analyse our genetic lineage, starting with Mums' side, grandparents, aunties then my Nan, who had very large breasts that bypassed both Mum and I.

As the years rolled on, my flat chest obsession became the least of my worries, but it never left me completely. When I was pregnant one of the highlights was growing breasts. After I gave birth, the milk came in and I really had a set! I admired them in the mirror because they were awesome; unfortunately they only lasted for a few short weeks. I felt grateful that my body returned to its usual slim shape within a few weeks of giving birth, and so did my boobs - only now they were even smaller than before. I was delighted that my body bounced back each time to slim easily after giving birth three times. It was only after my third child that I consciously watched what I ate and exercised for a few weeks to get rid of the extra weight gained. Once again my body returned to its usual size.

I loved turning thirty. Something shifted, as though all my insecurities lifted and my foolish, warped perceptions were replaced with gratitude. Overnight I developed a new attitude; now I was thankful for my slim body and proud of how it facilitated smooth, natural birth to three healthy children. My tiny breasts functioned adequately in the purpose they were designed for and they worked especially well during sex. My husband preferred small breasts, so what did I have to worry about? Nothing.

While my Mother wore padded bras, I never took to them, preferring to live with what I naturally had (or in my case, didn't have). That all changed one weekend on a road trip to attend a funeral with my parents and we stayed together in a motel. As usual when I was growing up, I would shower while Mum was getting ready; this time, her latest padded bra seemed to have taken a new direction in design appearing kind of "real." I was so impressed when I tried it on and checked myself out in the mirror from the side view, swirling around to the front view. I started raving about it to Mum and vowed to get myself one of these "wonder" bras.

When we returned home, I made it a priority to buy myself some of these fabulous natural-looking, padded bras. They were amazing except that the padding was synthetic, making me sweat. Also, I couldn't wear this bra with everything.

What I discovered from these few months of wearing padded bras is: I wanted to have breasts. I spoke with my husband to find out how he felt about me getting breast implants. He said it was up to me, supporting my decision either way. So I began my research. Although the internet existed, it was not common for surgeons to have a website, making it difficult to find "before and after" images. I found some, most of which were ridiculous-looking, appearing obviously fake. Some looked like tennis balls stuck under skin - this was not the look I was after, preferring a natural-as-possible appearance. The options for the actual implants were either silicone or saline. After researching surgeons, size, shape, recovery, prosthetics and - with knowledge of possible implications - in 2001 (when I was thirty) I underwent surgery to have 350ml of silicone-filled, round breast implants inserted via an incision on my breast line placed under my chest muscle. After all the swelling went down I was the very proud owner of C-cups. I loved them and I made no secret of it. If anyone I knew had the courage to ask for a look or feel, I showed them or let them have a prod!

My body image had naturally altered with my revived attitude anyhow, and these new breasts amplified my self-perception even more positively. I felt like these implants evened my body shape out. I was elated with the styles of tops and dresses I could wear with confidence - though best of all, I realised my bum was in proportion with the rest of me.

Body image is a funny thing. I do not know if everyone that suffers with it feels pressure to be a certain shape or size, or to look a particular way. I have known people of all sizes, shapes, and colour - and what I know without question is that confidence radiates from within. It is an energy emanating by how you perceive yourself. I have met girls who have had breast implants who had a different view of themselves compared to me. At times I witnessed extreme insecurity in some who, in an attempt to be accepted and loved, adapted their body to please or keep a partner. Some women underwent their procedure to fit a profile for their chosen career. Interfering with our physical appearance for somebody other than *us* is not ideal; in the end, we do what it takes only to feel good about ourselves.

Modern advances in medical technology allow people to change appearance at will; however, the reality is: if we have not addressed the core of where our self-esteem is damaged, no amount of plastic surgery or exercise and dieting to alter physical appearance will change how we feel inside. To allow changes that resonate deeply we have to understand our emotional psyche by exploring how we come to feel the way we do and who, if anyone, assisted in shaping us. Incidents throughout life can cause trauma that we may not realise is lurking; however, by understanding how deeply we were affected, we begin the process of accepting ourselves, flaws and all.

Accepting ourselves goes beyond physical appearance. It comes from feeling aligned with our traits and personality, both the amazing and the shadow side. We all have strengths and challenges innate in our psyche. Rather than covering up the less desirable aspects, peace arrives in leaps and bounds when we integrate as a whole.

My observations of people were not only for physical attributes; what intrigued me most was confidence. Being comfortable with who we are, no matter what our shape or size, is appealing. A charismatic energy beams from those who are content in their own skin and at ease with the person that they are on the inside, content with how they fit in this world.

From a spiritual perspective, our soul chooses the body it will inhabit while attending the School of Life. The appearance and body shape is decided by our soul to fit best with the lessons we have chosen to learn during incarnation. This includes disabled bodies and physical limitations such as being blind or deaf, and even those who have severe physical challenges. A blind person may have chosen to take notice and enhance the use of their other senses such as hearing and touch, enabling acute listening and perception of others through senses other than sight.

Someone who becomes disabled, perhaps ending up in a wheelchair, may be learning to surrender and accept their fate along with other aspects of life that able-bodied people take for granted. Their purpose may be to inspire others with their wise outlook.

It is hard to imagine that anyone would choose a body that is so physically disabled that they cannot move or are in a vegetable state. However, great leaps in wisdom can be achieved by being still. When accepting unconditional love and care from others, there is no choice except to receive without the ability to give back in return - at least not physically.

I have discovered when speaking to people who may be

deemed as less able, or people who have various ailments or disabilities, are usually wise beyond - they seem to see through the human judgments, teasing, and even unwarranted sympathy for what is essentially a misunderstanding of the purpose of life: meaning, we choose the 'perfect' body shape, physical challenges and appearance to assist with our mission. Our personal perspective and reaction to our own body type will poke our emotional bruises; yet, our body is only a vehicle to transport our soul through this incarnation. If you are insecure with any aspect of your physical body, the only way to alter that is to develop confidence and learn to be at ease with all the amazing things about yourself.

Confidence comes from within.

Other people do not view you through the same lens that you see yourself. Comments about your body will only affect you negatively if you already believe that you are not good enough; otherwise they have no effect. By the same rule, compliments will only resonate when you believe that you are already good enough.

Life Actions

1. In the past, has anyone made comments that altered your perception of your body?

2. What do you like about your body?

3. What features do you like about yourself?

**Connect with Toni and get
free resources to support you!**

www.ToniReillyInstitute.com/awake-bonus

CHAPTER 12:
OUT THE OTHER SIDE

My life has been nothing short of amazing so far. It may seem as though I centered on the trials in my life, and I did - because the big breakthrough experiences usually arrive through heartbreak, loss and major change. The reality is that my jigsaw puzzle is mainly happy or content pieces, littered with the odd rampant messy pieces, and all the parts shaped me. The emotionally trying pieces all evolve into wisdom for inclusion in the puzzle.

The Life Lessons I have learned so far and shared in this book are:

1. *To experience emotions is normal.* Almost every moment that we are alive we are feeling something. Happy, content, stressed, love, sad. They are very purpose for our existence. I always wanted to believe in life there was a great role to play, one of significance for each of us, and there is. No matter how many people we influence or reach in our lives, at the base line the interaction is to invoke feelings and emotions. They are paramount to this experiment called humanity.

2. *Accept what you cannot change.* Acceptance is the final stage where any form of grief that we suffer ends. Acceptance is the most empowering stage you can reach because you have broken through - no longer held captive by guilt, sadness or resentment, nor holding another person responsible for your feelings. Acceptance is as enlightened as we can be.

3. *Isolation creates leaders.* A brilliant leader does not rule with an iron fist, nor with fear, but with equality, seeing the poignant attributes in others and bringing that out in them to encourage confidence and acknowledgement. Positive leader attributes

require a person with empathy and compassion, who knows what it feels like to be excluded, unseen or misunderstood. The emotional maturity to lead with vision, compassion and vulnerability is what transpires from being bullied, teased and segregated.

4. *Relationships are our teachers.* I referred mainly to love relationships; however, all interaction with other people is a relationship of sorts. Everyday interaction always teaches us. Think of fuming in the car with rage at someone cutting you off at the intersection! You could let it spoil your day, or you could think more deeply and give them a break - because realistically, people don't usually do these things on purpose. Perhaps they were caught up thinking about an argument they just had, or they have a high-pressure task to take care of at work. Maybe they are daydreaming, wishing they were elsewhere. No crime, right? And nothing to get worked up about. Love relationships offer major traction to teach us about our insecurities and contribute to the reason we overcome them. If you find yourself still feeling bitter towards an "ex" try to take a moment to think about what they taught you - and vice versa. Remember the love that was there, or maybe still is. All relationships are teachers.

5. *Parenting theory does not reflect reality.* Because we never know how we would react or what it would be like in any given situation, our assumptions are just that: assumptions. Assumptions are a theories devised by our perspective on what it would feel like to us. Then we go further by assuming how we would react. The truth is: we do not know how we would react until we are in it. Think of someone who is held up at gunpoint: you might assume you would fall to pieces and be scarred for life by fear; whereas the person held up might feel calm, courageous and have empathy for the misguided gun-wielder. Think of someone who separates from their partner: one person may be devastated and do whatever it takes to save the relationship, while another may be relieved. Downgrading another person's emotional response by comparing what happened to them versus what you have been though can be intolerant. All feelings are valid. There is no right or wrong way to react or length of time to grieve. Tolerance is a gift, which means you do not have to fix anyone; simply let them feel the way they do.

6. We are energetically equal. I have heard so many statements, such as, "They vibrating at a different level," insinuating that others bring them down. Or, "I am old soul. They are a new soul." But on a soul level we are all part of the same collective of energy. There are no old souls, new souls, wiser souls, lower souls. We are all the same. And our soul energy is equal while we are in this body as well. We are simply here doing different things. The moment you rate yourself better or higher than someone else it creates a challenge for you to overcome. Hierarchy, levels and ascension are human inspired revelations which seem to exist even in the between life realm where we decide what we are doing while incarnated. Our soul energy is the collective where we are all connected, equal, with nothing to hide. We are all one. Differences only exist while we are here on earth to assist us by working through our challenges and experiences.

7. Our life is destined. When people talk about the phenomenon of *The Secret* or that you can manifest anything you want, I am certain that you only get it *if* it is part of your pre-destined life plan. Therefore, you can sit around all day manifesting to win the lotto and it will never happen (unless it is part of your plan!). What you will learn is a lesson – likely, that it takes action to achieve your dreams. Dreams and ideas are guidance put in your mind to follow through with. I believe that you are recalling your plan. This is the most empowering knowledge, given that we are driven by control. It allows us to trust compulsion, to follow through with action when the feeling to do so is strong and to sit back when the timing is not right. Following your intuition is how you work with your planned life map; when you do, life is no longer a struggle; instead, it becomes a flow of ease and grace, with outcomes that you know are as they ought to be.

8. Fate rules over free will. Fate is destiny. Your life map is set before you are born, just as it is for every other person. Free will is the human part of us - some call it *ego*. We need it to survive. We could not do anything without it. Synchronicity ensures that you are placed for every single thing that happens: to meet a lover, to be involved in an accident, to experience a miraculous recovery, to be reeled into drama, and to make choices or change your mind. Nothing happens unless it is fated, nor can you avoid what is fated. If you begin to look for signs, synchronicity is at play every moment, steering us, weaving us through our plan. You do not have to return in another incarnation to payback for what you did or did not do. You are simply having an experience. Everything happens for you to grow, not to punish you.

9. *We are volunteers, not victims.* It is easy to believe that we are misplaced here, especially when we feel like we do not belong. We assume that we could not possibly have agreed to experience such harsh experiences, but we did. If we have been a perpetrator in any lifetime, we come to experience the flipside of being the victim. We are, in effect, volunteering to assist the abuser to learn compassion as well. All situations are orchestrated to invoke emotional responses; that is the very purpose of humanity, to experience emotion. Therefore, the soul of a child who dies young has facilitated for the family members left behind the ability to feel grief and the associated emotional turmoil - which eventually leads to strength. The soul of the child (and anyone who passes) is unharmed, unaffected, when it leaves the body and transforms back to energy.

10. *Knowledge is human; Wisdom is soul.* Being creative and not academic inspired me to observe the difference between knowledge and wisdom. I arrived at the conclusion that knowledge is the gift of information passed on by people sharing what they have learned through education, while wisdom arrives through an intangible stream highlighting a philosophical perspective and outlook based on an inner knowing that defies logic or common sense. Think about an artist who writes songs or composes music. They learn to read music through the knowledge of others, yet their composition comes through a stream of untapped inspired wisdom that they transform into lyrics or music as a production for people to enjoy. We all become wiser through life, because we experience so much; we let go of control and move toward acceptance.

11. *Confidence comes from within.* This whole thing about "all the answers lie within" used to annoy me. I did not understand what it meant. What I am certain of now is that all of our persona is based on what is within. Inside our heart, hidden from view, is the centre for managing the way we show ourselves to others. When our confidence is damaged, only we can retrieve it. Think about my body perception where I believed I had a huge ass. People

would say, "You don't have a big ass!" but I could not accept their observation because I felt sure it that it was. It is so silly, but that is how we are. If we believe it then no one can change it. We can change our beliefs - oh yes we can! - and they might change through the influence of someone else; but the change will only happen because we personally believe something new.

Today I am far from perfect, but I love life. Helping people is the most rewarding mission of all. It never feels like work to lift someone's spirits and guide them so they can regain their confidence and feel worthy - like they *matter*.

Although I believe everything happens for a reason, it is *never* appropriate to offer this as comfort or consolation for what has happened to another person. This is a perspective that people arrive at on their own. Even if they do view what has happened as a crisis, it is for them to say, not us. Working with people means listening to them without interrupting or offering advice or a solution. Just listen. The greatest liberation you will discover is taking responsibility for your own life.

I established the Toni Reilly Institute to incorporate my SoulLife™ philosophy into modern intuitive personal transformation coaching, programs, seminars and certified training for others to learn to use these simple techniques and paradigms that make a real difference in people's lives.

By helping people help themselves, I assist them to create miraculous results that transform their lives by reclaiming their personal power, confidence and innate abilities that ripple out, improving their relationships, parenting skills, and career options.

Thank you for reading *Awake*. I invite you to try the array of useful tools available on my website so you can join our SoulLife™ community where we support each other. There are special complimentary offers there just for you! Join us at www.ToniReillyInstitute.com.

When we begin to see ourselves as perfect, just the way that we are, we can lighten up, stress less. and accept life as it is.

Life is filled with treasure, though we can forget that during times of crisis or reflective withdrawal. Take this heartfelt reminder to embrace the comfort of a hug, the taste of a delicious meal, the sound of music that makes your heart sing, or time spent being in Mother Nature. Let's celebrate connections with family and friends and focus on pleasing ourselves so that we are fully filled with love and kindness to share with others.

For those who are hurting, take comfort in the unlimited capacity of the human spirit to turn trauma into triumph.

And never say never, because maybe you will! Be kind, and when you can't be, lash out in writing, or confide in someone you trust; then return to kindness. Our natural state is love. We love to love and to be loved.

ABOUT THE AUTHOR

TONI REILLY is an author, speaker, seminar leader and internationally-recognized Past Life Regression Facilitator. She is the creator of SoulLife™ Coaching, Programs, Seminars and Training, guiding thousands of clients worldwide with her unique, intuitive approach to personal transformation.

Connect With Toni:
http://ToniReillyInstitute.com

Printed in Australia
AUOC02n1013080817
288388AU00007B/7/P